W9-BRE-015

Praise for Mike Ritland

"He's a good dude and doing great things for our four-legged heroes!"
—Larry the Cable Guy

"Perhaps most moving is how this level of trust plays a vital role in the inspiring and hair-raising stories that he shares about different SEAL handler-and-dog teams during deadly missions. . . . [*Navy SEAL Dogs* is a] high-interest offering."
—*Booklist*

"Special force SEALs are elite enough, but SEAL dogs [in *Navy SEAL Dogs*] are a breed apart. Fascinating . . . About time these heroes got the attention they deserved for a young audience."
—*Kirkus Reviews*

"*Navy SEAL Dogs* gives a unique insider account of the training and deployment of these special animals and their handlers. Ritland does a superb job of detailing these dogs in combat, as well as the bond between operator and K9."
—Howard Wasdin, former Navy SEAL and *New York Times*–bestselling author of *I Am a SEAL Team Six Warrior*

"After a stellar career in the teams, Mike Ritland has gone on to train working K9s for some of the most elite units in the US Special Operations community. If you want to learn about these amazing animals, the sacrifices they've made, and their effectiveness in combat, then read *Navy SEAL Dogs*."
—Brandon Webb, former Navy SEAL,
New York Times–bestselling author of
The Red Circle and Naval special warfare editor of sofrep.com

TEAM DOG

How to Train Your Dog—

the Navy SEAL Way

MIKE RITLAND

with GARY BROZEK

G. P. PUTNAM'S SONS • NEW YORK

PUTNAM
— EST. 1838 —

G. P. PUTNAM'S SONS
Publishers Since 1838
An imprint of Penguin Random House LLC
penguinrandomhouse.com

Copyright © 2015 by Michael Ritland
All photos copyright © 2015 by Michael Ritland
Penguin supports copyright. Copyright fuels creativity, encourages diverse voices,
promotes free speech, and creates a vibrant culture. Thank you for buying an authorized
edition of this book and for complying with copyright laws by not reproducing, scanning, or
distributing any part of it in any form without permission. You are supporting writers and
allowing Penguin to continue to publish books for every reader.

The Library of Congress has catalogued the G. P. Putnam's Sons hardcover edition as follows:

Ritland, Mike.
Team dog : how to train your dog—the Navy SEAL way / Mike Ritland, with Gary Brozek.
p.   cm.
ISBN 978-0-399-17075-1
1. Dogs—Training.   I. Brozek, Gary.   II. Title.
SF431.R58   2015   2014028704
636.7'0835—dc23

First G. P. Putnam's Sons hardcover edition / January 2015
First G. P. Putnam's Sons trade paperback edition / January 2016
G. P. Putnam's Sons trade paperback ISBN: 978-0-425-27627-3

Printed in the United States of America
10

Book design by Gretchen Achilles
Cover design by Nellys Liang

This is a work of fiction. Names, characters, places, and incidents either are the product of
the author's imagination or are used fictitiously, and any resemblance to actual persons,
living or dead, businesses, companies, events, or locales is entirely coincidental.

I would like to dedicate this book to my mom, Sandy.

She instilled in me the three most important qualities in dog training:

patience, consistency, and perseverance. Thank you for being

the shining example of what those look like. Love you, Ma.

Contents

Introduction

It all started with a black Labrador retriever named Bud. I was just a kid when we got him, and the connection between us was instantaneous. I realize now that our initial bond was a bit one-sided. I thought he was the greatest, and he thought, well, I couldn't say for sure what Bud thought. He liked whoever had a leash in hand and was willing to take him on a walk. He liked whoever fed him or offered him popcorn. He was willing to sit, stay, speak, come, and roll over when he knew that popped treat was his reward. He also liked whichever of the upright two-legged creatures fed him, allowed him to empty his bowels and his bladder, tossed him balls, and went with him to explore the outdoors, where his nose was nearly overcome by a series of odors that pleased and sometimes perplexed him.

My dad was usually the one who took Bud on his morning walks. I did the same in the afternoons when I returned from a day at school. Bud wasn't my own dog; he belonged to the family, and each individual member bonded with him to different degrees. It wasn't like I didn't have any human friends, but Bud and I really seemed to like doing a lot of the same things—being outside and exploring the neighborhood, doing anything but sitting around inside. We got along well, and the only real problem we ever had with each other was when my Rollerblade "walks" with Bud turned into off-pavement excursions, thanks to Bud's squirrel and rabbit obsession. I probably ended up looking like a bronco rider with one hand firmly grasping the leash and the other flapping in the breeze above my head.

Bud was an amazing companion, and nothing could beat coming home from a rough day at school and having him greet me with his tail thumping on the floor and him rubbing up against my legs, letting me know how glad he was to see me. That kind of display of affection is most likely the reason why, according to the American Pet Products Association, an estimated 47 percent of households in the United States have a dog. That brings the total number of dogs kept as pets in this country to 83.3 million.

That's a large number, and I wish I could say that every one of them is a well-adjusted, well-behaved, well-mannered dog. I'd also like to say that those dog owners have the best kind of relationship with their dogs. You've most likely seen some version of what I just described with Bud and me on my Rollerblades—a dog taking an owner for a walk, a hard-charging threat, a jumper, or a food stealer. Those actions don't make them bad dogs, just dogs with bad habits. That doesn't mean that their owners are bad people, just people with bad habits and a poor sense of their own authority.

No one in my family had formal instruction as a dog trainer; we just used the passed-along wisdom of having owned dogs before— the trial-and-error method combined with a few bits of old wives' tales. We were fortunate that Bud was good natured, and that my dad, who did most of Bud's early training, applied the same sense of discipline to raising Bud as he did to my two older brothers, my sister, and me. The only difficulties we ever encountered were with lax owners who let a couple of dogs wreak havoc on some of the neighborhood kids and dogs. For a long time, I had a healthy dislike for German shepherds based on my unpleasant interactions with a member of that breed who was the town bully. If you were to ask my dad, he'd tell you about an Airedale terrier who ran off his property and jumped Bud. My dad had to intervene, risking serious damage to himself, but he was able to separate the two of them. Bud was on the ropes and my dad saved him.

I share that story because it illustrates a couple of things. First, dogs are animals, and as much as we like to believe that their sweet and gentle nature rules the day, they do have a potential for violent action either when threatened or simply because their genetic make-up drives them to it. That's true for any breed of dog, though natural faulty wiring is somewhat rare. We never found out what set off that Airedale terrier. His owner was equally mystified. To hear him tell it, the dog had no history of such extreme boundary aggression, but something none of us humans could determine had prompted him to attack on that particular day and in that particular encounter. That said, the dog didn't just suddenly lose his mind, as I've heard many people say about their dogs—something in the dog's history caused him to respond to my dad and Bud as a perceived threat.

There's always a reason why dogs react the way they do—the trouble is that we aren't always able to discern that cause. This book will help you better read your dog, other dogs, environments, and circumstances to prevent those kinds of unfortunate events from taking place.

The second reason I told that story is because it illustrates the bond between man and dog. Dad was willing to get torn up in order to keep Bud from suffering the same fate.

It's beyond the scope of this book to go into the long history of human/canine relations, but at some point humans and dogs figured out that by working together they would enrich their lives in some way. I'd imagine that at some point early humans hunted prehistoric versions of dogs for food. That eventually transitioned into humans recognizing that dogs were also very good hunters and could be used as a tool rather than seen as an adversary. From the dogs' perspective, humans had something they wanted, too. They had resources like food and shelter. Most likely that came about as their natural scavenging efforts put them more and more in contact with us. When either we offered them some scrap or they laid claim to what we'd left behind, their natural associative way of thinking produced this equation:

Humans = benefit

Similarly, we arrived at the same conclusion. If dogs could help us collect more resources and also provide us with some security, then:

Dogs = benefit

In its simplest form, that is what a symbiotic relationship is all about. We both benefit from being around and interacting with one another.

Understanding how the initial relationship between dogs and

humans developed is the underlying basic principle of my dog training methodology. When you begin training a dog and developing a relationship with him, you are repeating the historical human/canine evolution in a compressed time format.

Keep in mind several points about this relationship that we've come to cherish:

- It didn't take place overnight.
- It is founded on mutual trust.
- It resulted in dogs doing more and more things for us that they weren't naturally inclined to do.

What's implicit in taking this approach is that human beings took charge of the relationship. Let me repeat that: Human beings took charge of the relationship. We saw dogs' natural abilities and then shaped their genetic destiny to a certain extent to meet our needs. Today, our needs are different from those of our ancestors, but that doesn't mean that the relationship dynamic should be inverted. We are still in charge. When I see so-called problem dogs, the problems stem from an imbalance of power in the relationship and not from the dog.

That is why it is important that you be in command of yourself, your understanding of dogs and their psychology, and my approach to training in order to be better able to control your dog.

Dogs are intelligent animals, but in comparison to humans, they are simple-association creatures. If you've owned a dog, you already know this to be true. If each time you pick up your car keys and then take your dog with you to some location and he has a positive experience, then he will come to associate that sound with some kind of reward. A dog doesn't understand that the keys are used to turn an ignition switch that results in an internal combustion engine propelling your car. What he understands is that the sound of the keys = good. In the same way, dogs came to associate humans with an expected future benefit.

We have given dogs enough resources to allow them to survive more easily, and we have gotten them to do tasks for us in exchange. If you look at any history of the modern domestication of dogs, you will likely come across discussions regarding the roles that dogs have played: hunting, tracking, herding, retrieving, and so on. At some point, because humans wanted to refine and preserve certain characteristics, breeding purebred dogs became an important exercise.

I've heard and read arguments that present dogs as nature's greatest con artists. That belief states that in exchange for being furry, cute, and charming, dogs have manipulated humans into providing them with lives of luxury. When you look at the last hundred years or so of human/dog interaction, it's kind of hard to find fault with the reasoning. I'd go so far as to say that many dogs in this country live lives of far greater ease than many human beings.

Because of my experience in seeing what dogs can do for us besides being good companions and a source of entertainment and affection, I don't buy into that con artist theory. After high school, I joined the Navy and eventually became a Navy SEAL. Bud was long since no longer a part of my life, and I had infrequent interactions with dogs. During my time as a SEAL, I was dating a woman who had what most people commonly refer to as a pit bull. (I prefer to use the term *bulldog* for the American Pit Bull terrier because of all the negative, and wrong, associations many people have with the breed.) One day she asked me to watch the dog for her while she was at work. When I took the dog for a walk, we encountered a raccoon tearing through the trash. The next thing I knew, the dog had basically turned the raccoon inside out. I was amazed at that dog's capabilities. I'd hunted with dogs before, bird dogs, but this was something different entirely. A fire was lit inside me, and I became very interested in hunting with dogs and seeing how they could test their mettle against prey.

I read everything I could about animal husbandry, breeding, and genetic theory and completely immersed myself, when I wasn't deployed, in the care, training, and capabilities of dogs. In a way, I was going back to an earlier place in human/dog history. While I liked dogs and all the qualities that they possess as pets, I also developed a greater appreciation for what they were capable of as tools to help human beings. In my case, at least initially, the application of this living tool was in hunting. That would also eventually evolve.

In the course of my training myself as a breeder, trainer, and user of hunting dogs, I was shaped by a couple of people's thinking. First was Dr. Stanley Coren, the author of *The Intelligence of Dogs: Canine Consciousness and Capability*. A professor of psychology, Dr. Coren was one of the first thinkers and writers to develop the field of dog psychology. His later book, *How Dogs Think: What the World Looks Like to Them and Why They Act the Way They Do*, also helped shape my approach to training dogs. The second person was Karen Pryor. Pryor also has written several books on dog training, and I think that her later book (after *Don't Shoot the Dog!: The New Art of Teaching and Training*), *Reaching the Animal Mind*, is far superior.

Being introduced to these two authors really opened my eyes, and their philosophy became the meat and potatoes of my approach to animal training, particularly as it relates to the psychological aspects. After reading those two books, I then read everything I could find by B. F. Skinner and Konrad Lorenz, among others in the field of animal behavior.

All that reading helped bridge the gap between the old-school notions I'd been exposed to in talking to other trainers to a more science-based approach. I began to better understand the anatomical differences between a dog's body and brain functions and our own and how dogs learn.

I was interested in understanding how a dog's mind works, how he perceives the world, and how a person could maximize his capabilities. I wasn't solely interested in getting a dog to be obedient and well mannered. There is absolutely nothing wrong with having those goals in mind, and that is the focus for this book. But I wanted to go beyond that baseline, first through hunting with dogs and later by training military working dogs (MWDs). The emphasis for me was always in testing the limits of dogs and their capabilities to be as beneficial to human beings as possible.

The first time I saw a military working dog in action was in 2003 as part of a SEAL team deployment in Iraq. I was a couple of years into my working with dogs, primarily bulldogs, when I was deployed there in the early stages of the war. A few weeks in, we were working in support of the 1st Marine Division. The city of Tikrit had fallen rather quickly, but pockets of resistance had to be rooted out. Clearing operations of that type, especially in an urban environment, are always fraught with danger. One day, members of our team were responsible for rooftop security while a group of Marines were conducting operations in the area. That evening a report came back that a member of the Marine unit had approached a small cavelike structure, with dirt piled around a small doorway. The Marine, with his explosives-detecting canine, approached the entryway. The dog worked his way steadily forward, nose to the ground. Suddenly, his tail started flagging and then he sat down immediately, his posture erect and his ears pointing to the sky.

As it turned out, that doorway was rigged with explosives, and if the Marines had tried to breach it without the dog having done his work, at least two or three of them could have lost their lives and several others would have been seriously wounded. Thanks to the dog, an explosive ordnance team was brought in, the threat was terminated, and the operation continued.

That was another lightbulb moment for me. I knew a few things about how dogs had been used in warfare throughout history. Seeing a dog saving the lives of my fellow soldiers firsthand put a dog's capabilities into sharper perspective. I couldn't do anything other than file that experience away at the time, but eventually, I contracted valley fever and was no longer able to be deployed operationally. So I separated from the SEAL teams, dusted off that mental file, and decided to combine two of my main interests—preserving our nation's security and working with dogs.

For the past fifteen years, I've been involved in the importing, breeding, and training of various types of working dogs. I worked for a time as a trainer of both dogs and handlers for the SEAL teams. Dogs I've trained have gone to work for the Department of Defense, U.S. Customs, the Transportation Security Administration, and the

Department of Homeland Security as well as to private individuals who want an added dimension of security in their lives.

To be honest, the kinds of dogs that I work with daily to perform these crucial tasks are not the types of dogs that are ideally suited to be housepets. Many of them can be, but more often, they should not be. When you train a dog to be a multipurpose military working dog—to detect explosives or to track and take down (detain) bad guys—you need dogs who are incredibly athletic and aggressive. I'll go into more about the term *aggressive* later, but for now imagine the kinds of dogs you've seen in movies and television who are able to literally bring down a human being, that kind of snarling, snapping, biting power that subdues an individual.

The purpose of this book is not to teach you how to make your dog into a Navy SEAL or other Special Forces operationally fit and skilled dog. Besides the incredible legal liabilities inherent in that, most of you reading this book don't want a dog who is that capable. The goal here, then, is a bit different.

I want to help you develop the kinds of skills necessary to effectively train your dog. This is a book about training you to be able to carry yourself like a Navy SEAL, to develop those traits within yourself to use in interacting with your dog, to develop your abilities to take command in a way that will help you most effectively control your dog.

As a consequence, I can't give you a step-by-step guide for every scenario that occurs when training a dog. I'd need to account for far too many variables in order to do that. A ten-thousand-page book likely wouldn't be sufficient to reach that goal. Explaining that many concepts and analyzing each of the particular elements peculiar to those situations would be like me spraying you with a fire hose after you told me that you were just a little bit thirsty. That wouldn't be pleasant or productive for either of us. What I can do is provide some step-by-step procedures to either prevent or address common issues. I will also teach you how to carry yourself in such a manner that you communicate to your dog by using your own body language.

The bulk of the book will be taken up with understanding how dogs think and behave, understanding what image you need to present to your dog, and how by effectively projecting authority, stability, situational awareness, problem-solving ability, and other traits—key components of what the military calls *command and control*—you will be able to develop the kind of relationship that will be most beneficial to you and to your dog. If you can master the skills, inhabit the proper mind-set, and understand a few basic principles, then training your dog will be relatively easy. Training yourself will be hard but worth it in the long run.

I've worked with lots of individuals who have asked me to help evaluate dogs, eradicate problems, and generally show them how they can restore the proper balance of command and control in their human/canine relationship. That relationship is based on trust and respect and produces a similar kind of bond or brotherhood that exists among members of the Navy SEAL teams. In my mind, that's the kind of relationship most of us want to have with our dogs. A lot of old-school methodology talked about dominance and reinforced the idea that the only way to be at the top of the hierarchy was by making a dog fear you. For example, there were many early advocates of performing something called an *alpha roll*. That consists of taking a dog in the earliest stages of training, grabbing him by the scruff of his neck, and pinning him to the ground to let him know who is in charge.

Yes, I do believe that it is important to establish your authority over a dog. Dogs want, need, and seek that kind of presence in their lives. But there are other, more effective, and decidedly more humane ways of achieving that goal. It is easy, in some respects, to get a dog to fear you, but it can be equally easy to get your dog to respect you. Just as is true in human relationships, a dog will have more respect for you if you make it clear that good behavior gets rewarded and poor behavior has consequences. That may seem obvious, but I'm constantly made aware that dog owners understand this in theory but fail to execute it in practice.

You may have noticed that I've not used the word *like* or *love* up to this point in describing the human/canine relationship. That's not an accidental omission. I've purposely not used those words because far too often I encounter people whose immediate response to a dog is to try to get that animal to like them. In doing so, they make fools of themselves in that dog's eyes, possibly put themselves in danger because they assume that how they treat their own dog is okay with a different dog, and mistakenly believe that because of all the nice things they do for their pet, the dog should obey their wishes and desires unconditionally.

If you take one concept away from this beginning part of the book it is this: Don't mistake liking for respect, and don't mistake obedience for trust.

At the risk of sounding like I'm trumpeting too loudly the connection I have with the Navy SEALs, I developed this training approach, which closely parallels the kinds of training emphases of the SEAL teams, because of one indisputable fact: It works. If you do what's demanded of you as a SEAL team candidate and later as a member of the teams, you earn tremendous rewards. If you screw up, you suffer the consequences—from getting hazed to being taped up to having your ass kicked. You don't get a free pass and listen to a lecture or have a report put in your file. You play by big-boy rules, and if you break those rules you'll know about it. Navy SEALs have an international reputation for a reason, and it all starts with that basic principle of expectations and consequences. You have to carry yourself a certain way, get the job done, be held accountable for your actions, and earn the trust and respect of your fellow team members. As much as Navy SEAL training emphasizes teamwork, when operational, there is one person in charge.

In working with your dog, you have to be that person in charge. Lives may not be on the line as they are in the teams, but the quality of your life and the quality of your dog's life are at risk. So is the bond that exists between you and your dog.

Without that bond in place first, training your dog will be a much more difficult task.

I distinguish between the areas of emphasis in overall training. In the first, you will build a trusting relationship and exert your authority to establish respect, manners, and boundaries. This will help you create the proper learning environment. Think of this as *command*. In the second, you will do additional behavioral and formal "obedience" training to maintain that authority, solidify your relationship, and truly enjoy each other's company. Think of this aspect as *control*. In the first, you will primarily use body language to communicate with your dog; in the second, it is all about using positive reinforcement enhanced by the use of a mechanical clicker to mark desirable behaviors that are immediately followed by positive reinforcements. In most cases, they are distinct phases, but in some instances you will work on the two more or less simultaneously, depending on the specific circumstances of your dog—his age, energy/attention level, and so on.

I believe many of you would like to have the ideal relationship with your dog that you've either seen on television or in a film or witnessed firsthand. Whether we are talking about a Chihuahua that stands six to nine inches at the shoulder or a Great Dane that reaches thirty inches in height, the theory and principles and practices that I advocate will help you take important steps toward establishing that ideal bond.

The responsibility for developing that ideal relationship is on your shoulders. The single most important aspect of building that relationship and firmly embedding your ideals of manners, boundaries, and skills is how you conduct yourself around your dog. That means from day one you have to develop and project a strong presence of authority and command. You have to exude confidence and authority. You have to take command of your body and carry yourself consciously and precisely; you have to use your voice sparingly and accurately as a tool, and you have to have control over your emotions and be able to move swiftly from expressing precisely modulated positive and negative states of mind, all in the service of presenting your most assured and confident self to your dog.

If you can master yourself you will then be the kind of master your dog is looking for and provide him with everything he wants and needs in his life.

There is no doubt in my mind that dogs are the most loyal creatures in the animal kingdom. I've seen and heard accounts of the amazing things they've done in combat and elsewhere. I've seen the kind of heartbreak that occurs when that human/canine bond is broken, whether it's when a handler loses a dog or a dog loses a handler.

Because I've seen how incredibly beneficial this relationship can be, and because I've seen how my principles and practices have worked with some of the most elite military working dogs as well as more typical housepets, I will say the following:

Many people get a dog because they see other people with good relationships with their dogs, or they see a puppy and he is cute so they want one, too. I want to make it clear that having a dog is essentially adding another family member, and it is not something you should take lightly or act impulsively on. Far too many times, people get dogs for the wrong reasons, or are in the wrong circumstances to achieve an ideal relationship with a dog. You have to understand that dogs take work, they take dedication, they take consistency, and you have to do the work to build that relationship and do the training *yourself*.

All that means that you have to make some sacrifices in your life, just as you do when you decide to bring a child into the world.

You can't outsource your relationship with your dog. If you truly want a dog to be "your" dog, and to bring to life the idealized vision you have of your relationship, then you have to put the time in and do the work and develop and execute the kind of work ethic required. All relationships, human and canine, require work in order for them to be fulfilling. The rewards that come from doing that kind of work far outweigh the expense of time and effort. Also, all relationships are dynamic, and you will have to continue to work through various issues and devise solutions to problems and make adjustments throughout your time with your dog.

No shortcuts here.

The bottom line is that if your dog isn't doing what he is supposed to or what you want him to, it's not the dog's fault. It's YOUR fault, for not properly communicating to him what you need him to do, not spending the time needed to train him properly, or not being observant enough to recognize early on when and how your relationship may be out of balance. Many people are too lazy to achieve the results they want. If having a spectacular relationship with your dog were super easy, everyone would have that and I wouldn't be writing this book right now.

One common excuse I hear all the time is, "I don't have the time." Well, I can assure you, you do have the time. What you don't have is your priorities in the order they need to be to have a great relationship with your dog. If it's not something you want to have, then you probably shouldn't own a dog. If it is, then rearrange the priorities in your life to be able to do that. With the right balance of trust and respect, calm and confident leadership that demonstrates that you are truly in command, and consistent positive reinforcement, all of you out there can have the relationship you seek with your well-trained dog.

We're both in this together, and if you love your dog, then it's time to turn the page and begin the work necessary to understand and implement the Navy SEAL way.

That means that if you get your mind right and get your dog's mind right, the right behaviors will follow.

ONE

Establish Yourself as the
Team Leader

When I arrived at the airport's cargo shipping area, I was met with angry eyes and a snarl.

"About time you got here."

And here I'd walked into the place, thinking that I was the one with the beef. I'd been at the airport for hours, waiting for a call to pick up what had been shipped to me. When the call finally came through, an exasperated voice said to me, "Would you get over here and pick up this f---ing dog?"

When I finally arrived, the guy who gave me the not-so-friendly greeting stepped to one side and waved his arms like a matador. Instead of a charging bull, what he was pointing to was a very large crate. Sticking through its well-chewed top was the very angry, snarling, and snapping head of a Belgian Malinois. He rocked the crate with the force of his movements.

Damn. We've got a live wire here.

I squared my shoulders and walked purposefully up to the crate, offering the dog a beef stick I'd brought along as a treat for my latest houseguest. Toby was a retired military working dog, and he was obviously not happy with being crated up and flown out to me in Texas. I could see his nostrils flaring at the scent of that meaty treat, but he seemed more interested in getting another kind of meat in his mouth.

Time for plan B.

Without making eye contact with Toby, I stayed far enough out of the range of his snapping jaws, got hold of the crate, and started dragging it across the floor of the warehouse. I was basically ignoring the dog, letting him go on his vocal rampage. I didn't have to imagine the look on the faces of the airline employees. I could see some of them staring wide-eyed while this Animal Planet–like nature documentary played out in front of them. Others just shook their heads and grinned while this man/beast parade float passed by.

I loaded Toby and his crate into the back of my truck and, once we were back home, let him loose into a kennel run at my facility. He paced a bit, alternately looking wary and pissed off. For the next seventy-two hours, I made no demands on Toby. Other than providing him with food, water, and treats, along with a healthy dose of verbal encouragement, I just let Toby be Toby for a few days. Every time I or one of my employees approached, Toby stared us down or assumed a defensive posture—ears forward, muzzle tensed, teeth exposed, tail erect and tensed, with his weight slightly shifted to his front legs.

Clearly, Toby was a dog who didn't want to be messed with. He didn't trust humans and, given his breeding and the kind of temperament often looked for in military working dogs, he was prone to biting.

The infamous crate that Toby destroyed during his flight to be retired to the Warrior Dog foundation.

HUMAN ERROR

Toby was only eighteen months old, far too young to be retired from the military. His age was part of the problem. He'd been rushed into training too early, he'd been forced to do too many things too soon in his training, and he'd also been given up on far too soon. Whoever had selected and trained him simply didn't have the ability to wait for him to mature and develop. Better put, they hadn't had either the time or the recognition that they needed to wait for the bond of trust between dog and human to mature before making demands on him. It didn't help that they'd employed compulsion-based corrective

measures as a way to coerce him into submission until he did what
they wanted; in fact, that was most of the problem. A very strong dog
at that early an age means you have to go about it like you are training a five-hundred-pound gorilla and not a canine. Toby responded
to the situation by biting a bunch of people and put a couple of them
in the hospital. He got bounced out of the program and was labeled
as being too hardheaded. I think I might have responded the same
way if every human being I had come into contact with for the last
four to six months had wanted to pick a fight with me.

In my mind, physically and temperamentally, Toby was an ideal
candidate to work as a Navy SEAL dog. He was as powerfully built
and athletic as any dog I'd ever worked with. His spirited nature also
ideally suited him to be a multipurpose military working dog. Dogs
his age who exhibit the kind of dominance that he does and have that
kind of strength are incredibly rare. I'd run into maybe a handful of
dogs in my life who refused to buckle under the pressure that we put
on them. Most dogs would come to the conclusion that this fight
wasn't worth it: *I'll choose to give in and do what you're asking of me.*
Not Toby. While his handlers deemed that he was just too much of a
handful, I perceived him as a dog who had everything going for him—
incredible genetics but inappropriate and rushed training. To a certain extent I understand that timelines are given from the powers that
be, and they are completely out of a trainer's control. However, there
are still much better ways to go about handling this type of situation.

Now Toby had been sent to me to be rehabilitated but not to be
returned to active duty. I had to ignore the shame in all that and
focus on getting Toby to trust people again, or perhaps for the first
time in his young life.

SLOW PROGRESS

In those first few days, we all began to notice changes in Toby's behavior and demeanor. Instead of stares, snarls, and barks, by day three of our making no demands on him, when we approached we were sometimes greeted by a wagging tail and attentive ears. The look of malevolence was gone from his eyes on those occasions. All was not completely okay in Toby's world, and we'd still note that intent gaze and postural changes every now and then. He'd gone from looking like he wanted to whip our asses to looking like he was just thinking that if it came down to it and he had to, he'd defend himself. A somewhat subtle change in expression and bearing, but an important one to be sure.

When we first noticed the tail wagging, I figured it was okay to proceed to the next stage. I started to let Toby out of the kennel run and into the fenced area for a kind of free play activity. Again, I began with essentially ignoring him or staying very neutral. But given his past, I didn't let my guard down for a second. I went about my business, but with my eyes and ears intently focused.

I carried a bag of treats with me and a couple of Chuckit! rubber tennis balls. I'd throw the ball and Toby would take off like a shot after it. I never tried to take that first ball from him. When I got his attention with the second ball and he let go of the first one, I then tossed the other ball. Repeat and repeat. Toby was tireless, and that energetic release each day seemed like something he really wanted and needed.

At the end of ball play, it was back in the kennel run. After numerous ball-playing routines, I let him keep one of the balls.

Eventually, at the conclusion of ball playing, I'd stay in the fenced area with him, walking around without any interaction. If he chose to come up to me, even just within close proximity, I'd reach into my pouch and offer him a treat. When he'd wander off, that was okay. The next time he came back, I'd repeat the process.

As I write this, Toby has been with us for a few weeks. At this stage, when we approach him to put a collar on him, he no longer tries to bite. The same is true when we touch his backside. We've worked with him in only the loosest sense of that word as it applies to dog training. We are in his presence, only sometimes interacting with him directly, feeding him and providing him with some play-time. The one thing we're working on is eliminating as many of the negative associations he has with people as possible. We need to break the old association of *humans only confront me and make me do things I don't like* and transform it into *humans are good and provide me with the things that I need and want.*

This will be a slow process and we've made some progress, but Toby is still not quite where he needs to be in terms of his sociability.

TAKING A DIFFERENT PERSPECTIVE

One of the key methods of my training is to put yourself in your dog's position and to try to see the world through his eyes. I could have looked at Toby and viewed him as a threat. From the perspective of most people, he was. He was biting people and therefore dangerous, and that made him no longer worth the time and effort for possible deployment. In another time, Toby might have been given to someone who would have employed very harsh tactics to break his spirit and show him that people were an even greater threat to him than he was to them. If even the most severe tactics didn't work to get Toby under control, he could very possibly have been euthanized.

I put myself in Toby's position and saw things differently. The previous relationship that Toby was involved in was fairly one-sided. People were making demands on him and asking him to do things in his training in unequal measure to what he perceived as his needs and desires. The few rewards he was getting did not equal the self-reward he earned by lashing out and going after people.

Just as some humans seem to take pleasure in bullying others and inflicting pain, so do some dogs. Toby was one of them. In fact, he had been bred and trained to subdue people, to inflict harm on them. Combine that with a high genetic drive toward outward aggression, his reactive defensiveness when faced with a perceived threat, and his past experiences with people using punishments to too great a degree to train him (and as a result, activating both his defensiveness and aggressiveness to a greater degree), and Toby lashed out.

Mainly, Toby wanted people to stop giving him a hard time. The only time they did was when he lashed out. As a result, he learned how to get what he wanted. As I pointed out in the case of my dad and Bud and that Airedale terrier, that other dog, like Toby, didn't just snap. There were reasons why he was behaving the way he did. Fortunately, I had some insight into those reasons and problem-solved so that I could determine a better way to get Toby to do what we wanted and lessen his desire to just be left alone to do what he wanted. He had too many good traits to be given up on.

Think of Toby's situation in terms of the human relationships that you have.

Imagine this. A new neighbor moves in and you introduce yourself to him. In the course of the initial conversation he asks if you would mind giving him a hand with a patio project he's working on. Somehow, he manages to manipulate you and coerce you into showing up the next day. When you arrive, there's a Ready Mix truck out in front of the house and the driver says that he was told to tell you that you needed to use the wheelbarrow to ferry concrete to the backyard. If you haven't gotten back into your car and gone home yet, when you're halfway up the steeply sloped quarter-mile driveway that leads to the house, you're really wondering now what the hell you got yourself into. Worse, when you get that first wheelbarrow up there, the neighbor starts to verbally abuse you, berates you for not being there earlier, questions why it took you so damn long to get that first wheelbarrow up there, and disparages your capabilities. Depending on your temperament, you will either walk away, tell the guy to screw himself, or even engage in a physical confrontation.

That's what it was like for Toby . . . but far worse.

Imagine instead that one of your closest friends, someone you've known for years and has done huge favors for you in the past, asked for the same help, promised and delivered pizza and beer, and genuinely thanked you at various stages. You'd likely be okay with the task at hand.

BUILD THE RELATIONSHIP FIRST

Obviously the demands placed on a working dog are different from those on a housepet, but the principle is the same. In my training of working dogs, I still put myself in the dog's position and understood that it was important to establish a positive rapport with that animal before I began making too many demands on him. That's just how good relationships work. While dogs are legendarily known as man's best friend, don't assume that from the very beginning you can instantly or even initially have that kind of bond. Friendships are built on shared experiences and the development of mutual respect and trust. You also know that all of your friends are not exactly like you are. You may share some of the same interests and points of view, but you aren't identical in every way.

A crucial factor in developing a positive relationship with another person is acknowledging the differences you have and making accommodations for them. The same is true with you and your dog. One of the key ways to develop trust and to forge a bond between you and your dog is to understand that dogs are animals who rely on the nonverbal components of communication to exchange information. We think that dogs respond to commands and that the verbal component, the words themselves, have meaning to them. That's not strictly true, of course. A dog doesn't understand the word *sit* in the same way that you or I do. He learns to associate those sounds with that specific behavior.

How?

When the dog performs the action that you want (in this case, sits), you reward him somehow—either with a treat or with praise or with some nonverbal cue that "says" to the dog, "That's what I wanted you to do." A dog doesn't have an abstract sense of what words mean. He simply comes to understand through repetition and association that a set of sounds and actions (from the subtle to the overt) are related to a behavior. Dogs also understand the tone of your voice and the volume of your voice, two other essential components of nonverbal human communication, and make associations based on pitch and volume. They also pick up on how you are holding your body and the smallest of gestures you make.

A SPECIAL CASE FOR THE WORD NO

If you've ever raised children you understand that using the word *no* to correct a child has multiple uses, intents, and subtleties. The same is true in working with your dog. Just as is true with other words that we utter, a dog doesn't understand *no* as it is defined, how it is used as a part of speech, and all the other more abstract aspects of language. He understands the negative associations of that word— don't do whatever it was that preceded that utterance. As with a child, your *no* conveys degrees of, forgive the term, *no*-ness. With a baby who is putting something in his mouth that he shouldn't— ranging from something that might have germs on it to something that is truly dangerous—you will use volume and intonation to indicate the level of seriousness of the situation.

From "No, that's icky" to "No! Put that down!" you naturally vary the qualities of your vocalization to suit the situation. Sometimes you do want to frighten your child to make sure he understands fully how important it is that he respond immediately. All this may be common sense, but it is worth noting that you have to have command over your tone of voice—one of the most important elements of communication with your dog. Suiting your tone to the situation is important, and your dog will pick up on the vocal cues and learn from your tone what is an absolute do-it-now, this-is-serious *no* from an I'm-warning-you-that-if-you-keep-that-up-then-something-unpleasant-is-coming-your-way *no*. If you use the first of those tones all the time, it will eventually lose its impact. Again, suit your tone to the occasion.

THE NONVERBAL COMPONENT

Voice and sound make up only a very small percentage of how dogs communicate with us and with each other. By an enormous percentage—I'd put it at about 98 percent—dogs communicate through body language. Experts in human communication estimate that somewhere between 60 and 90 percent of a message is communicated nonverbally. That's the old, "It's not what you said, but how you said it," line that we've all used or heard. Humans, because of our ability to speak, rely on sound as a primary means to communicate. However, facial expression, posture, eye movement, gestures, and spatial orientation all play a part in how we communicate with one another. We're conscious of the words we choose but frequently are not conscious of those other nonverbal parts of the messages we send. Often, the words we use are at odds with what our bodies are saying.

Since dogs can't speak, they use their bodies overwhelmingly as a primary means of communication. If you've ever seen two dogs interact with each other, you've seen this in action. One dog stands alongside the other and raises his head over the other's shoulders and behind the head. The other dog responds by straightening himself to stand taller, his ears erect, and his tail twitching. All of those gestures and body movements convey meaning.

TAKING COMMAND OF YOURSELF

If you are going to become your dog's best friend, you need to become better at not just reading your dog's body language but at "speaking" it yourself. Most of us are not fully conscious of the body we inhabit and what its various parts are doing at any one time. To be effective at working with your dog and to maximize your leadership potential, you have to become more conscious of your body and the head-to-toe signals you send.

The reason why this command of your body is essential is that dogs respect and seek (with a few exceptions) someone who will exert power and control over them. Dogs are social animals, and in the wild they existed in a highly structured and hierarchical society. While many dogs in the United States don't live with other dogs, they still have the inherited genetic tendencies from their ancestors, who lived in a strictly regulated social environment.

I cannot stress this point enough: Dogs respect confidence, power, and authority. And by dogs, I mean all dogs. I don't care how much of an alpha role any dog has assumed; when someone comes along who exhibits those three traits to a greater degree than they do, they will step aside. Mastering your voice and your body in interacting with dogs to project confidence, power, and authority is absolutely essential to the Navy SEAL way.

LEADERSHIP IS DIFFICULT

As I mentioned, Toby is a rarity, a one-in-a-million kind of dog who wouldn't back down. Most dogs who live as or are available to you as a housepet do not want to assume a leadership role in their social environment or your family. In my time in working with dogs, I can think of only four or five cases of dogs (and none of them were housepets) who were truly dominant, alpha-type animals. If you encounter one, you will know within thirty seconds that he is that kind of dog. He takes on that leadership role immediately, will take food or whatever else he wants from you, and if you try to stop him, he will attack you to get what he wants.

Assuming a leadership role is stressful for a dog that doesn't want it, and that's why we encounter so few willing to truly take on that position. Hardwired into every dog's brain is the idea that he fits somewhere on a scale of power and that someone will have more, relatively equal, or lower standing, status, or power within the group than he does. That gets reinforced from the very earliest days of dogs' lives as puppies with littermates. When they first encounter you after being taken from their littermates, they reenact the role that they'd assumed with the other puppies. Few dogs have the natural inclination to be a team leader. They expect that there will be one, and when one isn't present they feel stressed—the natural order of their lives has been disrupted. Some dogs adjust well to that while others struggle.

Think of your own experience in working in groups. If you're not naturally accustomed to leading and directing others, and you see that a task is not being accomplished because no one is taking control, then your stress level rises. Sometimes you reluctantly decide that you'll assume that leadership position. Sometimes you figure, What the hell. There's no leader here, so why not just make the best of it and do what's best for you. That's the approach that many dogs take in the absence of a clearly defined leader. A lack of human leadership is even more stressful for both you and your dog. You know what is needed to restore the natural order—you have to step up to fill the void of leadership that exists now that the dog isn't with his mother and siblings. You have to be the one in charge. Dogs, especially those at the top of the hierarchy, are motivated by self-interest primarily. In the absence of a leader, a dog will do what he has seen other top dogs do—assert control and seemingly do what he wants when he wants and how he wants.

As I mentioned in the Introduction, 83 million dogs live as a part of American households. Pet ownership is at an all-time high, and based on my experience and what I see taking place in our culture, the number of problems with pets is also at an all-time high. There are more dog trainers at work in the field, more television shows and dog training guides being published than ever before, yet the problems persist to a higher degree than ever before.

The obvious question is why?

THE FUNDAMENTALS AND FAMILY

My answer is that the lax, permissive attitude that exists in our schools, our homes, and our society in general has trickled down into how we interact with our pets. While there are some benefits to our living in a kinder and gentler society, there are also some huge drawbacks. That is particularly true as it pertains to dogs. Some people believe that it is possible to have a well-trained dog and to never have to physically correct that dog. I wish that were the case, but it's not.

Let me be clear. I don't employ and I don't advocate the use of any kind of unnecessary force. In the pages that follow, I'll make it more clear what kinds of physical corrections I'm talking about. But please understand this important point. If all you ever do is reward your dog for good behavior and you have no consequences for bad behavior, then your dog will not have a complete understanding of what's expected of him. In order for a simple-association animal to understand what *good* is, he also has to understand what *bad* is. Without any kind of context to cement his understanding of the most basic of principles between desired and undesired behaviors, between rewards and consequences, your dog cannot be well trained.

I make no secret of the fact that I learned so much about training dogs from being a parent and vice versa. I could save you some time and effort in reading this book by stating a few simple principles and leaving you to your own devices:

- Carry yourself confidently and act like a leader.
- Reward good behavior.

- Punish/extinguish bad behavior.
- Be consistent in the application of rewards and punishments.
- Keep emotion out of the equation.

Based on all my years of experience in working with dogs, I can imagine only a very few sets of circumstances where those five key principles wouldn't resolve any problem. If you want your dog to respect you, then you must execute those five points. Any dog will grow to respect you as a result of adhering to these basic guidelines.

WORKING IT ALL OUT

I also learned a great deal about working with dogs from my time as a Navy SEAL and in my time training and evaluating SEAL team candidates. As important as those five main principles are, they aren't enough to really help you develop the *optimal* relationship with your dog. They'll help you eliminate/reduce problem behaviors, but is that all you're looking for out of your relationship with your dog? Again, think about the kinds of relationships that you have with people. Is having them be problem-free the same as being satisfying?

Perhaps that is enough in a work relationship, but keep in mind that a dog is looking to you to be a replacement for the family he lost. At times, simple and therefore trouble-free family and close personal relationships may be a relief, but that isn't what you want long term and consistently.

As a result, you have to work a bit harder than simply mastering those five fundamentals if you want a deep and lasting relationship with your dog. In the SEAL teams, our instructors used the phrase *attention to detail* incessantly. We were reminded constantly that success was possible only when we were in command of every part of our lives. How we treated our bodies, our minds, our equipment, our brothers all mattered. Success was a result of paying attention to and mastering all parts of the whole. For that reason, to truly train your dog the Navy SEAL way, I'm going to make similar demands on you. Every aspect of dog ownership is an important part of the whole. If you cheat on one aspect of it, your relationship will degrade.

It's tempting to tell you that if you are looking for a shortcut or a quick-fix solution to a problem then you should turn to page X, Y, or Z. Training your dog the Navy SEAL way is more holistic than that. If you truly want the best from your dog and for your dog, you'll pay attention to every detail.

TRUST IS AT THE HEART OF THE RELATIONSHIP

Another element of taking command is building trust. A dog also has to trust you, and these two elements together form the foundation of any highly functional and mutually rewarding relationship. Dogs are looking for someone to lead. If you do that, and demonstrate that you will consistently and calmly provide them with the resources they need (food, water, shelter), the security they require (no abuse, consistent application of expectations and consequences), and the affection and relaxation/play they desire, then they will trust you and do what you ask of them. You'll be able to draw on a dog's inherent loyalty and desire to be a part of your world.

I know that many people refer to themselves as their dog's "mom" or "dad," and that some people cringe at that aspect of our anthropomorphic tendencies. I will also use those terms at times. For one, it's an easy and comfortable shorthand. For another, and far more important, I use those terms because they speak to a dog's needs and expectations and how important it is that you see things from the dog's perspective. Dogs are looking for the same kind of relationship they had within their family unit, so I use those terms to drive that point home.

Please do not mistake this bit of linguistic usage with how anthropomorphism often gets expressed—assigning human emotions to dogs' responses, dressing them in clothes that resemble what humans wear, and so on. Dogs do have a mother and father, more technically a dam and a sire, so my using *mom* and *dad* doesn't really qualify as part of our tendency to want to humanize dogs. It serves as a reminder of your role as authoritarian in your pet dog's life.

We likely take it for granted that a dog is taken from his mother and siblings at a very early age. Again, look at this from the dog's perspective. He is suddenly taken from the only environment he's ever known, a place where his needs are met and he is kept safe and secure.

What dogs are looking for and need at that point and throughout their lives is another family. Dogs didn't just exist in a "pack," they lived in a family, and the larger social network in which they lived mimicked that family hierarchy. A puppy or any older dog that you may adopt wants to fit into his new social group and is looking for leadership and guidance. From the very first day (and this doesn't have to mean you are working with a brand-new puppy; it is just your first day of training a dog), you have to let a dog know that this is your house and that you are allowing him to live there with you. My employees and I aren't making any huge demands on Toby that explicitly state his role in the pecking order. But that is exactly what we're doing in ways that are subtle to the human observer but loud and clear to a dog. We are letting him know who is in charge, without creating any conflict or getting physical with him.

PUTTING THE COLLAR ON: TYPES OF COLLARS

A choke collar is a training tool some use for maintaining command and control of your dog. In essence, they are chains that contract and expand, exert pressure on your dog's neck, and are somewhat useful at getting his attention and sending a signal, especially when paired with a short, sharp verbal command, to communicate that a behavior is not acceptable. Frankly, I don't like or use these types of collars for numerous safety reasons and would advise you to stay away from them.

Prong or pinch collars are similar in design to choke collars, except instead of the links being curved and smooth, an open piece of metal extends beyond the link and provides greater disseminated pressure. These collars are much

Examples of collars that you may choose to use, given the variables of your relationship and situation. From left to right: e-collar, prong collar, martingale collar, flat leather collar.

safer and more effective for getting a dog's attention if the intensity of correction needs to be at that level.

E-collars (electronic collars) deliver a mild to moderate pulse to a dog. Like anything, they can be used judiciously or abused. I have used e-collars on low settings, have tested them on myself, and can say that they are effective if other types of restraint collars prove ineffective with a particular dog. They do no permanent damage to a dog, are humane, and when used properly can maximize training time. Most important, when you use them, your timing can be perfect.

A martingale collar is made of two loops: one that fits

around the dog's neck and another (the control loop) that attaches to a leash. Because of this construction, it functions much like a choke collar but doesn't put the same kind of pressure on the trachea. It works well for those who want the attention-getting effect of a choke collar without the potential for harming the dog.

A flat leather collar is similar to a belt a human would wear. Because it stays the size you select, it doesn't serve well as a training tool. It serves well as a way to identify your dog by having a place to place tags and as a means to maintain positive control of your pet.

We are in control of when Toby eats, when he relieves himself, when he gets to exercise and play, and when he gets to interact with us. Also, we are showing him some respect by not making demands on him, not challenging him initially by making eye contact. We also aren't giving him the opportunity to do what he wants to do to most humans—that is, bite us. By not invading his space, respecting how he communicates through body language, and always approaching him from angles rather than head-on, we are telling him, "We get it. You're pissed off. We understand why you are. But we're not going to let you get everything you want."

As time progresses, we will make other demands and expectations clear to him and ask him to do more of the things that we want and need him to do. We will only progress once a level of trust is in place, so that he can understand the context and consequences of his good and bad behavior.

THE PSYCHOLOGY OF TRAINING

When it comes time to let Toby know that he doesn't always get to choose what he is doing and how he conducts himself, we'll rely on positive reinforcement as much as possible. Given Toby's history, we may not be able to keep with the usual percentages of positive feedback that we employ when training other working and personal-protection dogs, which is generally somewhere in the 90 to 95 percent range.

So just what does it mean to use *positive reinforcement*? The term comes from human psychology, principally the work of the psychologist B. F. Skinner. Skinner's work in studying human beings evolved to the point where he believed it was important to look at behaviors and their causes as well as the consequences resulting from those actions. His theory of operant conditioning added a dimension to the work of another psychologist, Edward Thorndike, which relied mainly on examining the effects of a behavior. Basically, Skinner observed that behavior that is reinforced tends to be repeated/strengthened, while behavior that is not reinforced tends to be extinguished/weakened. With that premise in mind, *operant conditioning* is a way to change a person's or, in our case, a dog's behavior by providing reinforcement after a desired action is offered.

Responses, or *operants*, can be one of three types: reinforcers, punishers, or neutral responses. If you want to strengthen a behavior, you reinforce it. If you want to weaken it, you punish or withhold reward for that behavior. Neutral responses obviously don't do either of those two things. If you use positive reinforcement with a dog, you provide some kind of reward (a treat, vocal praise, physical affection) when he does something that you want. Negative reinforcement isn't quite what you might think. It is the removal of some unpleasant reinforcer as a reward. Allowing your dog to get out of his kennel when he stops barking excessively is an example of this kind of reinforcement.

Punishment is essentially the opposite of reinforcement. You can either apply a direct unpleasant stimulus to a dog (physical punishment, a shock, strong tugs at a training collar) or remove a pleasant stimulus (keep the dog confined, take away something he has been chewing on or playing with).

More simply, think of it this way:

1. Something good can begin or be offered.
2. Something good can stop or be removed.
3. Something bad can begin or be offered.
4. Something bad can stop or be removed.

Think of the word *positive* as something that has been added to the dog's environment; think of the word *negative* as something being subtracted. You don't have to be good at math to remember + and – and what they represent.

Here's a quick chart to summarize how this works:

	REINFORCEMENT (behavior increases)	PUNISHMENT (behavior decreases)
POSITIVE (something added)	POSITIVE REINFORCEMENT: Something added increases behavior	POSITIVE PUNISHMENT: Something added decreases behavior
NEGATIVE (something removed)	NEGATIVE REINFORCEMENT: Something removed increases behavior	NEGATIVE PUNISHMENT: Something removed decreases behavior

Earlier I stated that we spent 90 to 95 percent of our time using positive reinforcement. That was a bit of an oversimplification. Now that you understand the terms better, I can say we spend only 5 to 10 percent of our time using positive punishment. That's when working with very strong and assertive dogs. With many housepet dogs, you may only rarely, if ever, use positive punishment. This is also all relative, in that reward and punishment are in the eye of the beholder. But the beholder here is the dog, not you. Again, we need to always see things from the dog's perspective!

Being able to read and evaluate your dog's temperament, and therefore what kind of reinforcers and punishers to use, is an essential skill and bit of knowledge to have. We'll look at how you and your dog differ in how you perceive the world in the next chapter.

TWO

Understand and Work with Our Differences

recently paid a visit to a friend of a friend who was having some difficulties with his family dog, Jonah. The owners had rescued him from a county shelter more than a year prior to my visit. By all accounts, Jonah was a good dog who presented few real problems to the owner except one. He was, the family claimed, very vocal and often barked at nothing. They sometimes thought that maybe Jonah was going blind since he would stare out the patio door and into the wooded lot their house sat on and bark tenaciously. They also wondered if this was potentially a sign of some other genetic disorder. Their major concern was that Jonah frequently woke them in the middle of the night with his incessant barking.

When I came to the door, Jonah gave me a robust greeting but appeared to be nothing more than a well-socialized and very friendly animal. I sat down on a couch and Jonah retreated to his bed nearby. A few minutes into our discussion about Jonah's problem, Jonah jumped up, ran to the door, and barked very loudly and persistently. He jumped in place, not making contact with the glass, but clearly was hoping that he could be let out.

I asked the owner to try to manage the situation the way he normally would. He walked over to the fireplace mantel, grabbed a spray bottle, then walked over to Jonah and sprayed the water in his face while saying "Quiet" in a very stern voice. Jonah backed away but continued to bark for a few seconds, before a second spray finally silenced him.

The owner turned to me and said, to both Jonah and me, "See. What did I tell you? There's nothing out there."

I walked to the door and looked out. Through the trees, I could make out a dark shape moving. Then I saw another. A small adult deer and a fawn turned toward the house with their ears raised and then bounded off. Jonah emitted a low growl and then slunk back to his bed.

WE BOTH SMELL A PROBLEM

I explained to Jonah's people that he had a keen sense of smell and hearing, and that most likely, whenever he was barking, it was because of something he scented or heard and not because of anything he saw. Most likely, by the time they got to the door and looked out, whatever Jonah had gotten a whiff of had either heard his barking and decided it was time to move on, or had done so independent of Jonah's actions. Jonah wasn't going blind and wasn't suffering from some kind of dementia—he was simply responding to a stimulus in his environment in the best way he knew how.

I'd heard of people using so-called quiet water before, and it would have been effective if at this point Jonah had ceased his barking immediately upon seeing the bottle. The reward he got from barking was greater than the positive punishment he was being administered.

I'll return to this scenario later to talk about how to break the barking habit, but for now, I want to focus on another aspect of the human/canine dynamic, because this is a good opportunity to better understand how to put yourself in your dog's position. As I stated previously, one of the most important components of building a relationship is to understand differences in perspective. This is what we're talking about in this case, with Jonah.

Dogs and humans differ a great deal in how they use their senses. When dogs bring in information to process, their predominant sense is smell, followed by hearing and then sight. For humans, simply flip that list of three on end and you have sight, hearing, and smell. While Jonah's owner's response to his barking, thinking that there was something wrong with him, is a bit extreme, it does point out how biased we are. As I dug a little deeper, I found out that, early in Jonah's tenure at the house, the kids in the family would run to the patio door along with Jonah, asking, in an excited state, "What do you see? What do you see?" Then they'd all gather, the dog and the little boy and girl, in a small circle of attention and affection. The adults told the kids not to do that once Jonah's barking problem got out of hand. Jonah's keen nose, his prey instincts, and the attention he was getting and the excitement that was stirred up with his bark and charge to the door outlived the change in the kids' behavior.

The parents were flustered because, in their minds, Jonah had no reason to bark. In Jonah's mind, he had every reason to bark. Even when he was being squirted with water, a clear signal that he should stop that behavior, he was still a little confused by the mixed message he was receiving. There's blame enough to go around, of course, but the point here is that if you understand better the cause of Jonah's behavior, something you deem undesirable, you can devise a solution that gets at the root of the issue and not simply one that addresses a symptom.

For humans, it's difficult to imagine what it is like from a dog's perspective to walk around in an atmosphere that is rich with scents. Estimates vary, but most scientists and researchers place a dog's sense of smell somewhere between 10,000 and 100,000 times as sensitive as our own. In a recent article that appeared on the website of the PBS television show *NOVA*, James Walker, the former director of the Sensory Research Institute at Florida State University, helped us visually dominant creatures get a better sense of how this inversion of senses works. He said, "If you make the analogy to vision, what you and I can see at a third of a mile, a dog could see more than 3,000 miles away." I know that in our bomb detection training of special operations or other working dogs, we're used to talking about a dog's capabilities in terms of parts per trillion, but those numbers most likely blur in your mind after a while. I hope that Mr. Walker puts that ability into terms you can really grasp. As humans we can recognize as many as 4,000 to 10,000 distinct odors. Dogs can recognize 30,000 to 100,000. So, the next time you're walking your dog and you get exasperated by his spending too much time sniffing around, remember that there's more out there for him to analyze than you can possibly sense.

A NOSE FOR MATING

Dogs have a second olfactory system that we don't have. At the back of their nasal passage lies an organ called *Jacobson's organ*. It detects pheromones, the chemical signal that each dog gives off to indicate readiness for mating and other elements of sexual activity. These chemical signals are processed separately from other odors, since Jacobson's organ has its own set of nerves that connect to the brain.

Alexandra Horowitz, the author of *Inside of a Dog*, did something similar but still kept the comparison in the olfactory realm. You can tell when your coffee or tea has sugar in it by taking a sip of it. Well, a dog could sense that same teaspoon of sugar diluted in a million gallons of water just by using his nose.

SMELL AND BEHAVIOR

So, what are the practical implications of this? Well, it would help you to know that dogs' brains and olfactory systems are substantially different from ours. With each breath a dog takes, part of that air is guided into the lungs for respiration and part of it (a little more than 10 percent) travels a separate pathway, where specialized structures filter and send signals to the brain for those molecules to be analyzed. To complete the circle, when a dog exhales, out of the side of the nostrils, the air that exits creates a vortex that helps draw in more air to be analyzed. That's an efficient system for bringing in olfactory data.

Anyone who has hunted with dogs or done any kind of tracking or detection work with them will recognize that a windy day is likely to change a dog's (as well as a handler's) behavior. With more and more different odors passing through a dog's field of smell, he is going to be, depending on your perspective, either distracted or hard at work. If you're involved in a training session and the wind is high, you can make your training very difficult or very easy depending on how you go about it. If the training area you are in seems to be permeated by swirling wind in a multitude of directions, you may have to either ratchet down your expectations or decide that it might be better to wait for a calmer day or to move to a different location to do the training—unless of course you're at an advanced level and purposely want to introduce this particular challenge for you and your dog.

Don't mistake a dog's preoccupation with a lack of focus or a lack of intelligence. Imagine yourself in a room where dozens of television screens are showing movies, sporting events, news, or other images. How easy is it for you to block all that out and focus on what the person sitting across the table from you is saying?

I once heard a teacher talk about a concept called "Look for the intelligence behind the mistake." I've been around a lot of people and a lot of dogs, and I've heard the opposite of that concept stated more times than I care to remember. "What's wrong with you today?" Few people take the time to consider the answer to that question and assume that something is wrong with the dog that is seemingly acting randomly. There's always an explanation, and recognizing how a dog's senses work and are different from your own is a good place to begin to investigate answers to that question. Don't assume that the dog is stupid or willful or whatever other negative pops into your head. Dogs are smart. Dogs sense and think differently from humans. Look for the dog's intelligence behind what you are labeling a mistake and you'll be surprised at what you might learn.

I HEAR YOU

Two different components of the physical structure of sounds are at work for all species—volume and frequency. We measure the first in *decibels* (dB). We quantify the second in a unit called a *hertz* (Hz) that measures the number of cycles per second a sound wave's peak travels. This is a simplification, but decibels measure the intensity of sounds that the human ear can detect. The quietest sound, near silence, is 0 dB and a firecracker is approximately 140 dB.

It is common knowledge that dogs can hear sounds at a higher pitch than a human can detect. A pup's high-frequency hearing develops over time, and generally, only by the fifth or sixth week past birth should you be alarmed by what seems to be hearing problems. For most of us, the fact that these sounds range from 40 Hz to 60 kHz (with each kHz—or kilohertz—denoting a thousand hertz) hurts our brains. To give you a better sense of what that means and how it relates to our ability to hear sounds in the approximately 12 Hz to 20 kHz range, here's a table to help you visualize these sounds better:

TYPE OF SOUND	INTENSITY/ VOLUME (dB)	FREQUENCY/PITCH (Hz)
Dripping faucet	20	130
Rustling leaves	5–10	1500
Human conversation	40	750–1,000
Human whispering	20	2,500–3,000
Dog barking	70	250
Baby crying	60	750
Vacuum cleaner	60	3,000
Lawn mower	100	250
Chainsaw	100	2,000
Firecracker	140	500
Gunshot	140	2,000
Siren	140	3,500–4,000

According to most audiologists, any sound above 85 dB can damage the human ear, depending on the number of times the person is exposed to that sound and for how long. At 100 dB, hearing damage can occur in as few as fifteen to thirty minutes of continuous exposure. At 120 dB, damage can occur within minutes, and at 140 dB instantly.

Humans' peak sensitivity to sound corresponds to the general range for speaking (approximately 2,000 Hz) while a dog's peak sensitivity is at the 8,000 Hz range—a point at which our ability to hear begins to degrade. Dogs can also hear sounds that originate from a greater distance than we can detect. This can be as much as four times as far away.

The implications and applications of this are obvious. Your dog isn't necessarily afraid of the vacuum cleaner, the lawn mower, gunshots, or nearby fireworks. He is just as likely wanting to keep his distance from those sounds because they are damaging his hearing or are painful. While some dogs lose their hearing due to congenital defects, as is the case with humans, far more have their hearing damaged or weakened by overexposure to loud noises. Many hunters wear ear protection to preserve their own hearing but don't take into consideration the long-term effect that exposure has on their canine companions. Of course, the joy that hunting dogs experience is hard to measure in comparison to what they might lose out on down the line.

I was basing my assessment of Jonah's smelling those deer rather than hearing them from the approximate distance away those animals were when I spotted them. That might not be true in every case. Jonah could have smelled *and* heard *and* seen those deer. Most likely, though, he caught their scent first.

SEEING THE DIFFERENCES

Here's a quick summary of the difference between canine and human sight:

- Because dogs have their eyes set farther to the side of their heads, their field of vision extends 240 degrees around them as opposed to a human's 200 degrees.
- Because dogs have something called the *tapetum lucidum* (a layer of tissue inside the eye), a larger pupil, and more

rods (one of the two types of photoreceptors, along with
cones) than humans do, they have something similar to the
capabilities that we have when using night vision appara-
tus. It takes approximately thirty minutes for our naked
eyes to adjust to darkness, whereas dogs adjust nearly
instantaneously.

- Dogs see best in low-light situations like dusk and dawn,
  while our visual clarity is best in full sunlight or bright
  light.

- Dogs have fewer cones in their retinas than humans, so a
  dog's normal visual clarity is 20/75 while ours is 20/20.

- As a consequence, dogs are less likely to recognize your
  facial features at a distance; instead, they rely on seeing
  your shape, but more importantly, because they have a
  superior ability to detect motion and body language, they
  recognize you based on physical gestures or actions.

- Because dogs' eyes are better at detecting motion, objects at
  rest are hardest for them to see—observe prey animals
  "freezing" to elude the predator dog.

- Dogs can see television, but because of something called
  the *flicker effect*, they don't see it with the same kind of
  clarity that we do.

Again, some of the implications of a dog's vision versus our own
are worth pointing out:

1. A dog uses his eyes mostly to confirm what his other
   senses have already told him. Telling a dog to "Look!

Look!" while pointing at something may therefore not be the best way to get your point across.

2. Ideally, the color of an object you want a dog to fetch should contrast with the background against which it will be visible.

3. Multicolored objects, particularly those that alternate bright and dark colors, are also ideally suited to a dog's visual capabilities.

4. Because a dog recognizes you by specific gestures and postures as much as by your features (particularly at a distance), developing specific actions to get a dog to recall (return to you) is particularly helpful.

A TOUCH OF DIFFERENCE

Because dogs communicate so much nonverbally, their somatosensory system, or sense of touch, plays an important role in how they interact with you and the rest of the world. This sense is the first to develop and is immediately functional at birth.

Dogs experience four different kinds of touch sensations: pressure, pain, temperature, and proprioception. The last of these allows beings to know where their limbs are within an environmental context. Dogs also have specialized whiskers called *vibrissae* that enable them to detect air currents, fine vibrations, and help them detect the presence of objects in the dark. These are located above the eyes, below the jaw, and on the muzzle. Thicker, more receptor-rich, and embedded more deeply than other hairs, they provide a kind of early-detection system for objects approaching a dog's face. Every hair on a dog's body has a receptor nerve, making them highly sensitized, but a dog's nose has an especially high concentration of sensory nerves. From tip to tail, then, dogs have a specialized and acute nervous system, including their paw pads, which can detect vibrations.

PUTTING THE MUZZLE ON MUZZLES

A word about muzzles and gentle leaders. A muzzle is sometimes necessary, but any time you place something around a dog's head, you could be impacting sensitive areas of his body. Not only could this stress the dog, but you may be interfering with the natural functioning of his sense of touch. As with anything, you have to use these devices advisedly and weigh the benefits and risks, but I advise against using them for most housepets, with exception to injury/medical situations. In most instances, the root of the problem isn't being addressed—only the symptoms you should be dealing with.

Touch is an important part of communication among human beings. Think of how differently words can come across when someone places their hand on your shoulder or arm. In what probably has its roots in a dog's earliest memory of the security he finds in his mother's touch, gently stroking and caressing a dog has the positive effects of reducing pulse rate, lowering blood pressure, and taking the edge off states of arousal or anxiety. In a real demonstration of the symbiotic relationships between canines and humans, we experience many of the same positive effects when in contact with dogs.

A QUESTION OF TASTE

If you know much about dogs, what you likely assume about their being indiscriminate eaters is partly true. Because dogs aren't as visual as we are, they eat things that we deem disgusting based on how they look. It's also true that dogs have fewer taste buds or receptors than we do, but we both recognize the same basic four tastes: bitter, sweet, sour, and salty. Compared to us, dogs have far fewer salt-specific taste buds, and some of their taste receptors pick up compounds found in meats and may be responsible for a dog's preference for it.

That said, while dogs are carnivores more so than omnivores—they eat both meat and plant-based foods—that is likely an adaptation born out of necessity rather than desire. The receptors that respond to sweet tastes are likely a part of our intervention in their evolutionary process. In Chapter Four, I'll spend much more time talking about nutrition.

The main takeaway here is that a dog's sense of taste is based much more on smell than sight. Consequently, what you perceive as gross could be incredibly appetizing to a dog. Basing judgments solely on human perceptions and preferences does a disservice to your dog and is another example of many people's failure to acknowledge and accept the reality that their dog is an animal.

A NOT-SO-DIFFERENT LANGUAGE

Understanding how dogs' senses function and influence how they view the world and behave is just one part of that respectful appreciation and utilization of their tremendous capabilities. Another way to express that is to return to a subject I touched on briefly earlier—understanding their predominant language: body language.

Let me preface this discussion with a disclaimer: I'm always hesitant to make statements that seem to imply that anything is true across the board. Even when it comes to information about a dog's senses, there is variation among individual members of the canine species, different breeds, and individual members of that breed as well as crossbred dogs. Some dogs may not have acute senses of smell, or their hearing may not be strong, or they may have some other differentiating quality.

What follows is a general description of typical canine methods of communication using common body language movements, poses, and expressions. Because we are going to be touching on issues that relate to safety—aggression and other topics—you can't use this information solely as your guide to how to interact with dogs and feel comfortable with your expectations. There are always variables that may dictate other actions.

Much of what I am about to discuss here and in later chapters in talking about the specific issues of training a dog have to do with you developing something called *situational awareness* (SA). Navy SEALs have this concept drummed into their heads and bodies from day one. Having well-developed situational awareness can save a SEAL's life. When you are interacting with dogs, a life-or-death situation will be rare, but the risk of being bitten and injured is ever present.

A common way of thinking about SA is to simply think of paying attention—to *everything*. That means paying attention to yourself and your body and the signals you are giving off and receiving. It also encompasses your environment—your immediate surroundings, your location within a prescribed bit of space as well as the larger context of that space. Imagine that you are in a room. Where you are in that room, what items of furniture are nearby, where the doors and windows are, and so on are things that you note and keep in memory. Expand that awareness out from that room into the building, extend it beyond the building to the nearby structures, and increasingly move away from yourself, and you get an idea of how complex situational awareness can be. You have to understand and acknowledge environmental factors like weather, time of day, and amount of available light as well as other people, objects, and animals, and note specific details about them.

When you are working with a dog, your situational awareness should be focused on you, how you're responding internally to a situation, how you're responding externally to a situation, how your dog is responding externally, and what that may tell you about his internal state, as well as environmental factors.

How does body language fit into this? Well, obviously, your dog can't speak to you to tell you how he's feeling internally and what he's perceiving in the environment. He's going to rely solely on his situational awareness, which in most cases is much more highly refined than yours, to help clue you in to what's going on. Also keep in mind that given the different degrees of acuity of each of his senses, he's going to be aware of things that you may not. And he's going to communicate that to you the only way he knows how: through body language.

READING YOUR DOG

Dogs can communicate more than just whether a situation is safe or unsafe. They are highly expressive animals and we can learn to read their states of mind and body, their motivations and desires, and predict their actions with greater certainty by paying attention to them and their responses. In order to present this material, I have to do it in separate parts. Keep in mind that the goal of situational awareness isn't to focus on just one individual component but the whole. Noting your dog's eyes will give you only a part of the picture; assessing other elements like his posture, tail position, and so on will give you a more accurate assessment of what he's thinking. Like humans, dogs communicate a great deal with their heads and faces. Each of the component parts of a dog's head can serve as a form of communication.

The Eyes

While the size and shape of a dog's eyes can vary, when the eyes change from their normal appearance to larger or smaller, the dog is cluing you and others in about his internal state. Larger eyes indicate some state of fear or stress. Smaller eyes can also mean the same thing. Squinting is frequently an indication that the dog is experiencing discomfort or pain. Where your dog directs his gaze is equally important to assess. Rarely will dogs look one another in the eye. That is a threatening action when displayed toward another dog; however, if your dog does this to you and you do it to him, it is most often by itself not a threat. You have to assess the rest of the facial expression, whether it is relaxed or tense, whether teeth are bared, and so on to know if that stare has some other intent.

Many trainers use the term *whale eye* to describe a dog who is not looking at you directly and as a result exposes much of the white part of his eye. If you've ever seen a dog with an object in his mouth and you approach him and he shifts his attention from chewing to assessing you and guarding that object, you've likely witnessed a whale eye.

People frequently remark on the upturned lips of certain breeds as a "smile." That's another of our anthropomorphic tendencies, but there is some small truth in it. A dog whose mouth is slightly opened to completely closed is likely to be relaxed. When stressed or frightened, and also when signaling submission, his mouth will be closed but there will be some tension in the lips—drawn back slightly and upturned. An exaggerated yawn also is an indication of a stressed state.

If there is a dog smile, it is more of a grin of submissiveness. That's the most extreme expression of their ceding dominant status. Their lips are pulled back and up vertically and reveal their front teeth. This is different from baring the front teeth and their canines and is seldom done without other indications of submission such as slumped body posture. When a dog shows his teeth and retracts his lip as a sign of aggression or warning, frequently the muzzle will be wrinkled, the eyes widened, and the hackles raised along with stiffness and other changes in the body.

A dog's aggressive pucker, when his lips move forward and he exhales through his mouth and his lips expand, is another warning sign to back off.

The Ears

Unlike humans, who don't communicate much at all with their ears and have little control over their movement, dogs have eighteen different muscles that aid in manipulating the ears. Dogs have a variety of ear shapes, and the most common are dropped (Labrador retriever), pricked (German shepherd), semipricked (Shetland sheepdog), or long hanging (basset hound). When relaxed, your dog's ears will be in their natural state. When his attention is focused, they'll be raised. When the ears go up and ahead, that's a sign of higher aggression or alertness. Ears that are pulled back slightly can indicate the opposite— that a dog is inviting attention. If the ears go flat completely or away from the head, that can be another sign of heightened nervousness, or it can mean submission. The ears always need to be looked at in conjunction with the rest of the body to determine their communication.

The Tail

A wagging tail isn't always a sign of openness. Like the ears, depending on the breed of the dog, the tail will be in a different position naturally. Any variance from that natural or neutral position sends a signal. In other words, anything from a gentle side to side to a frantic beating back and forth indicates levels of pleasure or joy. Some dogs even move their tails in a circle like a propeller to indicate their good mood. The height at which your dog holds his tail is also an indicator of mood or state of attention/arousal. A lowered tail with an alert, upright body posture is generally associated with a state of confident relaxation. A lowered tail with a slightly crouched body posture means anxiety or submission. A tail tucked between the legs and other shrinking movements of the body are greater indicators of that same mental state. A raised tail is a signal that a dog is alert. Flagging the tail, having it raised and moving side to side, is an intensified state of alertness and also possibly a threat, especially when combined with other threatening signals like growling and baring of teeth. Generally, the higher and more straightened a dog carries his tail, the more he is stating how high he is in social standing.

Some dogs also bristle the hair on their tails, making them look larger, or may bend them in a position different from their natural state—these two can often indicate that some possible act of assertiveness is the next step.

In many ways, a dog's use of his tail is perhaps his most common form of expressing intent and state of emotion. Human beings do similar things with their faces and bodies, but since we live in a culture where looking at someone eye to eye is both the norm and a way to put someone else in their place, we may focus too much on what's going on with a dog's front and not enough on what's going on in the background.

Posture

Three simple words: small, normal, large. Those three words encompass how your dog will hold his body and present his size. When a

Normal posture: a comfortable, confident dog.

Dog starting to make himself smaller in a submissive fashion.

Dog further making himself smaller and more submissive toward his owner.

dog is happy and playful he reveals no tension in his body. When scared, a dog will appear to have shrunk in size. Lowering himself to the ground or otherwise decreasing his height is another way of communicating fear or stress. A dog who lowers his head is saying the same thing. Also moving the weight to the back legs, instead of evenly distributed over all four, will allow a dog to retreat more quickly and states the dog's uncertainty.

An assertive or dominant dog will try to make himself look larger. Raising himself up, appearing to stand on the tips of his toes, and shifting the weight forward to the front paws—which makes it easier to lunge—all indicate some level of aggression. The dog is also issuing a challenge to other dogs, indicating his belief in his authority over them. Putting a paw on the back or shoulder of another dog while in this stance is an added reinforcement that lets the other dogs know his intent to be the top dog among them.

Keep all this in mind when I turn the discussion to how you should carry yourself in the next chapter.

The most obvious signal of submission to another dog is lying on the ground and exposing the underside. When a dog does this to you, you know that he believes that you're the one in charge—even if you do end up being the one to scratch his belly.

Much of this is common sense, and I won't go into too much more detail here. If you've observed dogs at play, you've seen the difference between their relaxed natural state and an aroused, attentive, and assertive state. One of the most common moves dogs make is what is referred to as the *play bow*. Bouncing into position, lowering their heads, and sticking their butts up in the air signals a readiness and

Different body positions communicate your intent and authority to the dog. Notice the start of submissive body posture from the dog in response.

Dog submitting completely to his owner: underbelly exposed and tail tucked.

willingness to engage in playful action. Taken individually, those signs might indicate something completely different.

Again, because dogs are living, breathing animals who exist in a dynamic environment, there is no one hard-and-fast rule that applies in all cases. That's why your ability to pay attention and develop strong situational awareness is so crucial not just to your and your dog's safety but to your development of a bond of respect based on your authority.

THREE

Set Yourself Up for Success with Proper Selection

In the teams, we were constantly reminded how it was important to focus on the small details as well as to see how those details fit into the larger picture. That may seem contradictory, but it really isn't. When you truly have a sense of how a process works, you look both at the near term, what's happening right now, and what that will lead to down the line.

That applies to every bit of dog training. If you can adopt that as part of your thinking—details and big picture—from the moment you start to consider having a dog as a pet, you'll go a long way toward establishing the kind of relationship founded on authority that is necessary. I spent a number of years as a trainer of Navy SEALs as well as the dogs they employed.

DOING FOR VS. DOING WITH

At an event for my previous book, a man came up to me to get my advice about a situation that had developed with his two-and-a-half-year-old German shepherd. He and his wife had been on a list to rescue a German shepherd, but the timing hadn't quite worked out like they'd planned. They got the call that a dog was available, but they were going to be leaving on vacation the day after they could pick up Karl. They had their hearts set on Karl, so they made arrangements with a neighbor/friend to watch him while they were away for ten days.

As the man told it, by the time they'd gotten back from their trip, Karl had completely bonded with the other family. He reluctantly went home with the original owner, and according to the man, he and his wife treated Karl very well, providing him with all his needs.

I asked how the neighbor had treated the dog that made the bonding so intense, and the man replied that the neighbor worked from home and went hiking with the dogs several times a day. I suspected that this was a case where Karl, who had lived in a city environment after being dropped from a police department training program, was a dog who liked and needed that kind of activity. The man told me that he and his wife loved Karl, but they both worked and it wasn't possible for them to get Karl much exercise.

They lived in a semirural area on a dead-end road, where all the neighbors had dogs who didn't always have to be on leashes. In some ways that was ideal, but in others it was frustrating. Every time they went out with Karl and he wasn't on leash, he would run to the friendly neighbor's house. Karl wasn't happy when he was dragged back home, and the man felt like Karl still clearly preferred to be with that other family. The man and his wife were a bit embarrassed, and short of keeping Karl on a leash all the time, they didn't know what to do to discourage Karl from hanging out with that other family.

Without seeing them all in action, I suspected that Karl was voting with his paws. By going over to the neighbors', he was showing his preference for being with people who could be more active with him. The neighbors tried to discourage Karl, but those early experiences with him were hard for Karl to forget.

This story illustrates that for many dogs it isn't so much about what you do *for* your dog, but what you do *with* him. Most of Karl's needs—food, shelter, water—were being met, but his need to not be alone and to be out in the world seeking and playing were not. We've all heard someone say the line, "I do and I do for you and this is the thanks I get?" Well, keep in mind that, for dogs, doing *with* often matters even more than doing *for*.

Any kind of training, whether it is human or canine, involves having a precisely focused image of what you want the end product to be. That means having an image of how that individual will behave, what he is capable of doing, how he will respond to new situations and stimuli, how he will respond to a command structure, and how he will fit in with others in the group. As an instructor of humans or a trainer of dogs, you also have to formulate an image of the process it will take to produce that desired end result.

As you might guess, the SEALs have a pretty good idea of what traits to look for in potential candidates for the teams, what interests they have, what kind of mental capacities they possess, and so on. Interestingly, members of the SEAL teams are far more diverse in their background than you might imagine; those core skills and traits they possess—thinking quickly on their feet, mental toughness—come wrapped in a variety of physical packages and with a host of educational, professional, and personal backgrounds.

The Navy SEALs have one goal in mind: to get the best and train the best for the purposes in mind. There were many ways that the guys got to the point where they were able to meet our rigorous standards and graduate from Basic Underwater Demolition/SEAL (BUD/S) training and then integrate themselves into the existing teams.

You need to apply some of the same kind of near-term/long-term thinking and image setting into your selection of a dog. Keep in mind what I said in the Introduction. A dog is looking for certain things from you—he wants to be led, and he wants to be a member of a family group. As a being with greater thinking ability/processing power, you need to have an even more firmly established set of expectations about what you want in a dog than the relatively simplistic desires and expectations that a dog has. Think about why you are bringing another being into your household. While it is great that some people want a dog because they feel bad about the number of stray or sheltered animals in the world, it is equally okay to be selfish here. In the long run, it is not better for a dog if you aren't properly prepared or knowledgeable about how to fulfill his needs and optimize your relationship with him. Think about what you want to gain from having a relationship with a pet dog.

SELECTION IS CRUCIAL

I can't emphasize this point enough. In most cases when I've been asked to intervene in problem-dog situations, what I see instantly is a mismatch—such as either a slightly built person or an elderly couple who have a seventy-five-pound high-energy dog who they can't walk without being dragged along. Those people are physically incapable of exerting enough force to stop that dog from moving—a necessary first step in getting a dog to walk properly on a leash. That's just one example of how better selection could have resulted in a better relationship.

Setting yourself up to be successful is of paramount importance. The Navy SEALs know what they are looking for in team members. They have a specific skill set that an individual must possess or be able to develop in order to earn that trident. None of that has to do with how those individuals look, their educational background, or their family history. It is all about functionality. What can this individual do? How will he perform under stressful conditions?

The good thing is that many of the men in the Navy self-select. They know what is to be expected of SEAL candidates and say, "That's not me." As a result, only a small percentage of active-duty naval personnel even attempt to qualify. Among those that do choose to enter BUD/S, some fail to meet the initial physical performance standards, and then even more fail to make it through the challenges of the qualifying school.

You have to think about the selection of your dog in a similar manner. You have to know exactly what you are looking for in a dog and then go through as rigorous a selection process as possible to identify the best candidate. Once you do, as the SEALs do, you then put that dog through a proven program of training using the best methods and equipment possible to produce the types of behaviors you want, because a dog can't self-select or may not let you know immediately that he's not a good match for you temperamentally, physically, or socially.

Too often I hear people talk about the temperament of a breed. "Labrador retrievers are mellow," for example. That may be true of individual members of that breed, but it is absolutely not true across the board. The same is true for negative associations with a breed. So don't seek or drop from consideration a dog because of mythical breed personality traits. That kind of profiling is inaccurate and may result in getting a dog that doesn't meet your needs or your expectations. If a Labrador retriever is too large a dog for you to handle, then disqualifying the breed because of a physical trait is a better reason to remove the breed from consideration.

Do the important work in advance of getting a dog, and your life, and the dog's life, will be much better for that effort.

DOG BREEDING AND OUR RESPONSIBILITIES

Many good breeders act responsibly and care deeply about not just their own dogs but the species. They are to be commended for employing good breeding practices and ensuring that the line remains as healthy as possible.

We also know that many irresponsible breeders are operating in backyards and running so-called puppy mills.

We can't legislate good breeding practices. We can try, but those efforts will be largely ineffective as a result of supply and demand. Obviously, we have an oversupply of dogs in this country—look at any shelter and that point will become obvious. The demand for dogs is great, and as a result, the market has been flooded. Too many dogs are destroyed every day in this country as a result of our collective vanity and self-interest.

What can you do about that? Do what I suggest and be as selective about your dog as possible. That means doing your research, being certain of your needs, and not getting a dog from a shelter or from even a reputable breeder on a whim. That means not selecting a dog based on what's trendy, or what's cutest, but basing your selection on what you have envisioned as the ideal functional relationship between the two of you. That means putting in the work necessary to make sure that you create that ideal relationship and not just settle for whatever is easiest.

ENVISION WHAT YOU WANT

People who employ working dogs have to develop a specific set of criteria for the dogs they acquire. They emphasize what a dog must do in order to be useful. While I am a member of the camp that places utility at the top of the list, you also shouldn't completely discount what you want to do with your dog as a main requirement for selection of a housedog. Dogs are meant to be active and are happiest when they are doing something. That doesn't mean that they have to herd sheep or other animals. They don't have to work in search-and-rescue operations; they don't have to detect and apprehend bad guys.

We domesticated and bred dogs and altered the course of their genetic destiny with amazing speed and variety to suit our needs. If you look at any book that describes the various dog breeds and classifies them into groups, those descriptions nearly always begin with some description of the kind of work or active tendencies these dogs have. I have a book called *The Book of Dogs*. It was published in 1927 by the National Geographic Society. Here's a description of the greyhound: "Developed originally for great speed in pursuit of antelope, gazelle, desert hares." At the time it was published, that was still a fairly accurate description of what a greyhound's intended use was. Those dogs had a distinct appearance, but as time went on, what they could do was superseded by their appearance. Yes, greyhounds were and are raced, but today, with the exception of specialized breeders who raise them to compete, they are bred primarily to conform to a specific set of appearance standards. The same is true of the Russian wolfhound. It has that name not because it resembles a wolf, but because at one point in its history, it was being bred to hunt down or to protect flocks from that predator.

FORM VS. FUNCTION

We've clearly placed form over function when it comes to choosing dogs for the home. Maybe this is because we are such a visual species ourselves, but I think it's a shame, and some breeds are being ruined because of this tendency to stress how they look over what they can do. Bulldogs, more commonly known as English bulldogs, are a prime example of this overemphasis on physical appearance, particularly within so-called purebred dogs. Among the laundry list of physical ailments that English bulldogs suffer from—eye and ear problems, skin infections, respiratory ailments, immune system and neurological disorders, and problems with moving, eating/digesting, copulating, and bearing puppies—many are attributable to breeding practices to produce dogs with what are considered desirable physical traits.

I don't want to belabor this point, but I also don't want to make it seem as if this problem doesn't extend to all breeds, because it does. In general, the overemphasis on appearance versus functionality can cause problems when appearance and expectations don't match well. Even if you do some hard thinking before selecting a type of dog that you want, and if you think about the things you'd like to do with your dog—Frisbee competitions, agility trials, playing fetch, hiking, running, swimming—but are overly swayed by the desire to have a certain breed because of how it looks, you could end up with a dog who isn't functionally suited to the activities you want to engage in.

This is true of purebred dogs, mixed breeds, dogs from a puppy mill, or dogs from a reputable and responsible breeder. However, you lessen your chances of a mismatch if you do that long-range/short-term thinking I mentioned earlier.

THE GENERIC DOG

Because of breeding practices to suit the desire to have dogs look a certain way rather than to breed them for the characteristic capabilities for which they were originally selectively bred, many so-called purebred dogs today retain few of their original skills or have them in a more diluted state. Therefore, if you enter the selection process thinking that you want X breed of dog because it is capable of A, B, and C, which suit the interests you have in pursuing with your dog, there's no guarantee that you will get a dog who possesses those traits or is a willing and suitable companion for those activities. The same is true if you enter the process considering only dogs in certain classifications that the American Kennel Club (AKC) uses—sporting dogs, hounds, terriers, and so on.

In terms of capabilities and function, what we see today is a generic dog. I know that is a loaded term implying lower quality, but I use that expression specifically in regard to what dogs do and how they live their lives in comparison to their ancestors. Just as we've evolved to the point where few of us do true physical labor, the same is true of canines. The term *companion animal* wasn't really around even twenty-five years ago, and that has become a dog's main work these days. I, too, believe that they are ideally suited for that job and enjoy having them play that role in my life.

I'm not alone in my belief that a more active dog is a happier and healthier dog. Temple Grandin, the renowned animal science researcher and advocate and author of the books *Animals Make Us Human*, *Animals in Translation*, and others, has written and spoken at length about animals and their behavior and treatment. She advocates for animals of all types to be allowed to act naturally, to engage in behaviors that they would have performed in a nondomesticated state. She relies heavily on the work of Dr. Jaak Panksepp, a neuroscientist at Washington State University. For all animals, she recommends, "Don't stimulate rage, fear, and panic if you can help it, and do stimulate seeking and play." She goes on to talk about the lack of seeking and play in most dogs' lives, their lack of interaction with other dogs. Because of that lack of stimulation, a result of most dogs being alone for much of the day and allowed to express their natural behaviors only briefly, "many cattle have better lives than some of the pampered pets." That's a provocative statement, but I think it is one we should all keep in mind in assessing our expectations when considering bringing a dog into our lives.

Knowing what you expect out of a dog and knowing what he needs to have a better quality of life from the beginning of the process will make the training methods I advocate even more effective. Even though your vision of the dog you want to have may seem very different from mine, the same principles apply in the early stages of evaluating a dog's suitability for your purpose. While I have strong ideas about what that purpose is, I can't impose them on you. I can, however, take you through the selection process so that you get a dog that will be the best-case scenario to meet your individual needs.

GETTING YOUR MIND-SET RIGHT

Before we get to the specifics of that process, I want to take a moment to turn this discussion around again to focus on you and not the dog. If a dog is looking for someone to take charge and exert authority over him in order to not burden him with that responsibility, then you need to carry yourself a certain way. I go back to something I said in the Introduction about wanting to be respected over liked.

Think about the kinds of introductions and greetings you've had with people and the variety of ways in which they've interacted with you. How would you respond if you met someone for the first time and they rushed up to you, hugged you, tousled your hair, jumped up and down, and generally acted like you were the greatest person on the face of the earth? Would you think that person's assessment of you was valid? Would you like that kind of physical contact? Would you think that this was a great starting point for a long-term relationship? Would you have respect for that person?

Most likely the answer to those questions is, "Hell, no!" You'd probably take a step back and think that there was something wrong with this person, that they had some kind of need for attention and affection that was well outside the bounds of what you'd be willing to provide and would most likely make you absolutely exhausted down the line if those needs remained the same or grew stronger.

I can't tell you the number of times I've seen people present themselves like that person I've just described when they first encounter a dog. They want to be liked, be loved, be best friends forever instantaneously. Every now and then, they're going to encounter a dog who responds well to that, but the signal that they are sending immediately is this: I need you!

What kind of dog is going to be attracted to that kind of greeting and that message? A needy dog. It feels good to be wanted and needed, but keep in mind that dogs who express that kind of initial enthusiasm for you are indiscriminate. They respond to just about anyone and everyone that way. What's going to happen down the line when you have a dog like that who expects that everyone wants to greet him and be his best buddy and give him attention? You're going to have a lot to do to train that dog and establish boundaries about who, when, where, and how he should interact with people other than you. Just because you enjoy having a dog jump on you and lick you doesn't mean that everyone does.

This brings up another aspect of keeping a near-term/short-term focus. A part of responsible dog ownership is recognizing that not everyone has the same set of expectations and desires about how a dog should carry himself that you do. In addition to thinking about what you want out of a dog—and I did say that you can be selfish—you also have to factor in how that dog will coexist with your spouse, your children, other family members, houseguests, and neighbors. Few of us live in complete isolation; dogs are social beings like we are, and projecting how any dog you select will fit in with you (small picture) and within your entire social context (big picture) is an essential part of the evaluation of a dog's temperament.

Encouraging that kind of over-the-top display of affection is the complete opposite of how you should present yourself to an unfamiliar pup or dog. You are the one who is making the decision. You are the one in charge, and how you carry yourself into the situation and what signals your body language sends are something that any dog will recognize and decode immediately. Do you want to concede the position of power in that relationship immediately? Absolutely not.

When meeting new dogs, stand nonconfrontationally and just ignore them. Let them show you who they are; don't force it.

THE FIRST ASSESSMENT

The first part of a dog's temperament or traits to assess is sociability. That assessment will be based on one-on-one interaction with the dog in as neutral an environment as possible. That means only one dog at a time in a space that is not overloaded with other environmental distractions. Whoever is responsible for the dog should allow you to take the dog to some neutral space to do this kind of assessment. I would consider any kind of reluctance or refusal to allow you to do this a huge red flag and would most likely walk away from that situation.

If your dog will live within a larger social group, I suggest that you and anyone else who will be living with the dog, and who is of an age to be able to do these kinds of assessments, "interview" each dog individually. Too many people at one time can overwhelm the dog and may give a false picture of his sociability. Later on, you can compare notes, narrow the field of candidates, and decide whether to proceed. This is true for all the traits mentioned here.

Whether you are going to a shelter, a pet store, or a breeder's property to view a dog, you need to present your best, most authoritative self to the dog. That means that your posture is erect with shoulders back, your facial expression is neutral and composed, and every other part of your demeanor is also in command. That doesn't mean being robotic, but it does mean being seemingly indifferent. You've likely seen someone enter a room who gives off an air of confidence, a kind of nonchalant self-contained assurance that says, "I know there are other people in the room, but I'm not here to please you, impress you, or try to get you to like me. I'm just being who I am, and you can take it or leave it." Those are the kinds of people who command respect and attention.

PUBLIC AND PRIVATE DISPLAYS OF AFFECTION

Many people want a dog who will be openly physically affectionate with them. That might mean having a dog sit in their lap, accept hugs, or otherwise physically interact with them in a way that humans feel is an expression of love. Not every dog will tolerate or enjoy that kind of contact. Just as different people have different levels of comfort with physical touch, the same is true for dogs.

If your vision of the ideal dog includes that kind of contact, then it is important to assess a prospective dog's sensitivity to that kind of touch. Most pups will be willing to be held and held close, but often only to a point. Handling a dog in a fashion that is close to the kind of contact that you expect to have down the line will give you some indication of just how willing he is to have his movements restricted.

CONFIDENT. SELF-ASSURED.
SELF-CONTAINED.

Problem dogs are often handled by being shuffled along from one temporary caretaker to the next until someone finds that dog's disruptive behaviors acceptable. Don't start that cycle. Taking an overly social dog who wants to greet everyone with the same enthusiasm as he does his owner and teaching him when that's acceptable and when it's not will require time and patience. Again, dogs need consistency, and while you can teach a dog the difference among individuals and their preference for a level of affection or physical contact, you will be assigning yourself a difficult task. If you desire that kind of affectionate relationship, then take on a dog like that, but just be aware of the consequences and responsibilities that go along with that choice. And, please, don't pass that dog along later or blame him for acting in a way that is consistent with his nature and that you initially rewarded and welcomed.

I would want a dog who is cool and confident at first. Just as you can contain or extinguish overly social behaviors in a dog, you can also get a dog to be warmer and more affectionate down the line. Once you develop that bond of trust, the affection will flow from there. Think about your personal relationships. How many of them started out gangbusters and then leveled off, and how many of them evolved over time into deeper and better ones?

On the opposite end of the spectrum is the fearful, hesitant dog who upon first meeting will shy away. That dog will also be difficult to deal with over time. Those issues of fear and mistrust can be overcome, of course, but the same kind of patience, and perhaps even more, is necessary to get that skittish dog to engage in the kinds of activities and relationship that you seek. If you want a more distant relationship than the typical kind of overtly affectionate one that many people seek in a dog, then you are probably still better off with a dog who is confident than one who is fearful. Fear and mistrust issues, which are rare in puppies, are not insurmountable but can be tricky to deal with down the line.

Dogs' levels of social interactivity exist along a spectrum between the extremes I've mentioned in detail. A dog who is more middle-of-the-road will present fewer challenges along the way. You have to decide what is acceptable and desirable, formulate a picture of what kind of responses and behaviors you want, and assess the dog from there. Also, the scale that you might mentally use to judge a dog's sociability will be different when looking at a puppy versus a juvenile or adult dog. Rarely will you see a puppy who is completely cool, calm, and collected. You'd be making comparisons among littermates in all likelihood, as well as using your own experience with other pups.

ACTIVITY/ENERGY LEVEL AND PREY DRIVE

In addition to determining how social a dog is, assessing his activity/energy level is important. I make a distinction between sociability and activity/energy level. A highly social dog seems to crave your attention—he will come up to you frequently, follow you, jump up at you, and so on, all in an effort to get affection or attention from you.

That doesn't necessarily mean that same dog is high-energy or high-activity. It may, but one doesn't necessarily follow the other. A dog with high energy moves around a great deal, is reluctant to quietly lie down, and seems to give off a generally more energized vibe than other dogs. Those dogs' motivation for being energetic and active isn't tied to interaction with you and the gratification you give them.

TEST YOUR VOICE

Since dogs are nonverbal animals, you should evaluate how they respond to the tone of your voice. In talking to a dog, you should use your normal tone, which will test his hearing more than anything else. Then drop your tone lower and use a more stern voice and note how the dog responds. Do the same with a more high-pitched/excited voice.

Generally, you can arouse a low-energy dog with higher pitches and calm a high-energy dog with lower tones. Seeing how responsive a dog is to those nonverbal clues will give you some sense of what to expect down the line when you begin more formal training.

Given what I do for a living, many people say to me that their high-energy/highly active dog is a kind of spaz who needs a job; he needs to be a working dog. I don't believe that's the case. Here is where another term comes into play. *Prey drive* in dogs is distinctly different from high energy and frantic activity. Prey drive is a more focused exertion of energy in pursuit of objects—toys, balls, small animals, and so on—than just mere burning of energy. Prey drive is a genetic factor expressed in a dog's behavior. Prey drive cannot be taught. Either a dog has it or he doesn't.

As I sit here writing this, one of my housedogs, Rico, is lying sprawled across his bed. If I were to get up and grab a ball, he'd look up at me and notice what I was doing. It would take me waving the ball in his face, teasing him with it, getting it moving, to get him up and moving. Once I did that and then ventured out of the house and threw the ball, you'd witness a Jekyll-and-Hyde reaction. That somewhat laid-back/sleepy dog would transform into a supersonic beast tearing after that ball. Rico is probably a bit of a rarity in that he is not a super-high-energy dog with a high prey drive. More often than not, the two are paired.

As the term implies, prey drive is all about pursuing and taking down another animal for food. Since we provide dogs in our homes with food, most of them express their prey drive in the pursuit of toys, sticks, and balls. It is rare for dogs to have prey drive for other dogs, and especially for humans. We look for that willingness and desire to take on people in evaluating dogs for our special operations forces, but it is unlikely that you would ever encounter a dog with that kind of prey drive in your search for a housepet.

Think of a high energy/high activity level as misguided energy—the pursuit of movement and activity simply for the sake of burning off energy. That's not necessarily a bad thing, and strong prey drive is not always a good thing. If you are interested in having a dog who is a good running companion, a dog who is willing to hike all day with you, go cross-country skiing, or engage in some kind of endurance activity with you, then you want and need a dog who is on the high side of the activity and energy scale. Couple that with high prey drive, and you'd likely have trouble controlling that dog's impulses and safely engaging in running, cycling, hiking, cross-country skiing, and so on. That doesn't mean you want a dog with zero prey drive, or that you couldn't control that dog, but a dog with high prey drive is probably the most challenging type of dog to deal with.

How do you test for prey drive? I recommend that you bring a ball or a toy with you when you go to meet prospective dogs. Again, in as neutral an environment as possible, isolate yourself with the dog and present the ball or the toy. Judge how he responds to the sight of the object. Does he ignore it? Show interest in it? Jump up and down excitedly and try to grab it? Next, put the ball or toy in motion. How does the dog go after it? What does he do with it after he pursues it? Does he bring it back? Does he engage in "kill" actions—shaking it as if trying to snap the neck of a captured animal? Though I hate to make generalizations, dogs who shake objects in a manner that simulates what they would do to dispatch prey generally are on the high end of the scale for prey drive.

If your vision of the ideal dog is one with whom you play fetch or tug-of-war, I should warn you that if a dog doesn't exhibit the desire and motivation to engage in those activities with you from the start, it is highly unlikely that he will develop that trait later on or that it can be "trained into him." Conversely, if you don't want a dog who is into chasing after objects, then I'd say you'd be doing a dog who is highly motivated to do that a disservice by trying to extinguish that drive. You'd also probably have some trouble doing so. Prey drive is inherent in some dogs, and dogs with high prey drive, the ones whose bodies literally shake and shiver with anticipation and who stare at you with that intensely focused gaze and a "Throw the damn thing already!" expression are on the high end of the spectrum. A dog who sprints after a ball, pounces on it, maybe even crashes through, crashes over, or evades obstacles in order to get it, is at that same level for a housepet.

Again, know what you're getting into and be prepared to deal with the consequences of taking on a dog with a high expression of that trait.

Strong prey drive doesn't equal a good dog and a low or nonexistent prey drive doesn't equal a bad dog. It all depends on what you want and what you envision your relationship to be like and what activities you want to engage in. You have different human companions who match your interest levels in activities to various degrees. You can find a dog who will without any kind of intervention on your behalf meet your requirements better than others.

AGGRESSION AND ASSERTIVENESS

Handling and training the kinds of dogs that I have for all of my adult life, I may have a different perspective on what constitutes aggression than many other people—including other experienced trainers—have. That doesn't mean that I recommend as a housepet a dog that intends to harm another dog or a person for no reason other than the desire to inflict hurt. That is a rare trait in a dog, and

I believe that what many people see as aggressive tendencies are not aggression but what I would term drive (food or prey) or in other specific instances, possessiveness. With the proper training and with you establishing the kind of authoritative position necessary to deal with any type of problems, those traits can be controlled.

When a dog has a toy or a ball in his possession, he is viewing it as a resource similar to food or something else he needs. How willing is that dog to surrender that object? If you've been around dogs, you know that different dogs present different behaviors when you try to take a resource away from them. The growling and the change in stance or posture can be mild or strong. Some dogs surrender a ball or toy easily; others want to engage in play with you and make those guttural sounds as a part of that activity, while others will snarl, snap, and put on a greater display of their desire to retain what they possess. That is also termed *resource guarding*.

Sometimes they have what I would call dangerous possession. One of the dogs I care for, a rehomed working dog, broke my wrist because whoever had him from day one of his training never taught him that releasing a toy or ball was a good thing. This dog doesn't have as strong a prey drive as some of the others, but he does possess that heightened possessiveness. Most likely, instead of being rewarded when he gave up the object, he was punished or choked off a ball before he released it, and that was a frustrating experience for him.

A puppy who, as early as twelve weeks, growls when you approach his food bowl or when involved in a game of fetch, is expressing a learned behavior. In dealing with his littermates and his mother, he got his way by making those sounds and acting out.

When assessing a dog, engage him in some kind of play with a ball or tug toy to see how possessive he is. Don't drop a dog from your list of potentials, particularly a puppy, because he shows signs of growling or other possessive behaviors. Extinguishing that behavior is a relatively easy fix with pups. They've only just learned that behavior recently, so it is generally easy for you to help them unlearn it.

THE MOST MISUNDERSTOOD BEHAVIOR

You're walking your dog and suddenly you hear barking and the pounding of paws. Fortunately, the sounds are coming from a fenced yard. The dog inside the fence comes up to that barrier and begins barking, bares his teeth, raises his hackles, and has his ears straight up or slightly forward. You're probably thinking that dog is aggressive. I would say not necessarily. Most likely, that dog is fearful and what I call thin-nerved. He is not intent on harming you, but he is willing to defend himself on his property and feels somewhat threatened by your presence.

To me, that is a crucial distinction. True *forward natural aggression* is offensive in nature—in other words, not prompted by anything you or another animal did to incite it. A dog who perceives that he is being threatened, has been somehow literally or figuratively backed into a corner, and then defends himself is not expressing forward natural aggression. Offensive and defensive assertiveness are two very different things. A dog who is willing to defend himself, or a dog who gets uncomfortable and frightened and reactive and ends up trying to bite someone, is far more typical than the truly offen-sively aggressive dog. Too often what I view as defensive assertive-ness gets labeled as aggressiveness.

A dog who jumps up and tries to take a ball from you, a dog who snatches food from someone's hand, a dog who bumps up against you, or a dog who growls when you approach him while he's eating and/or you move to take a resource away is not being aggressive. He is not intent on inflicting injury on you.

Are these behaviors desirable? No. They are, however, learned behaviors that can be modified. True forward natural aggression can be harnessed, but it takes someone with an enormous amount of experience to deal with that kind of dog. Those dogs are rare and you would most likely never encounter them at a shelter or from a quality pet breeder. The important point here is to not be warned off a dog as a potentially suitable candidate for you if he shows some kind of assertive behavior.

Many dogs have what is termed *barrier aggression*. I don't like the use of that term, but for the sake of this example I will use it. Dogs are territorial, just as people are. In terms of body language, humans have what communications theorists term our various *bubbles* or spaces. Those are the distances from other people in which we feel comfortable. Depending on the environment and the people with whom we are engaged in an interaction, that space will vary. The same is true with dogs, but because of our history with them, the guarding functions they performed for us, and how they inter-acted within and between groups of dogs, they have a more height-ened sense of protective territoriality than we might.

A dog who charges a barrier, as dogs in any neighborhood across the country do, is expressing that sense of boundary protection and guardedness toward other dogs. You can, and should assess this, but keep in mind that it is a learned behavior and not a sign of natural aggression in 99.9 percent of cases. To do this, have the dog you are assessing in his neutral environment. Then ask to bring another dog into that environment. Most shelters or breeders will have a fenced area. Have the target dog inside the barrier and walk another dog along the outside of the fence. Observe how the dog you are interested in responds to the presence of another dog.

A dog who demonstrates guardedness is a dog who you will have to work with to eliminate that tendency. If you decide that's not something you want to deal with, then simply move on.

LITTERMATES AND PARENTS

In the puppy evaluation process, I think that it is tremendously important to be able to see as many members of the litter as possible, and ideally both parents. Many breeders may tell you that only a certain dog is available to you and you may have to deal with that fact, but it shouldn't limit you from seeing how the dog being offered to you interacts with the rest of the pups and with his mother.

In many cases, when viewing a litter, you will see that one or possibly two of the dogs seem to be the most assertive. People often make the mistake of believing that dog will be the strongest of the bunch. I don't believe that there is any correlation between what some would call the alpha dog/leader of the pack among a litter of puppies and his relative strength of temperament as an adult. In fact, the reverse is often true. What you should be looking for is a pup who interacts fully with the others and engages in playing, wrestling, and tussling. Again, it would be rare to see natural forward aggression in a pup, but if you do, you should immediately eliminate that dog from consideration unless that is what you are truly looking for. Also, any dog who does not seem sociable with the other pups, the one who might be seeking isolation in the corner of the environment or who otherwise seems standoffish, is one that you also should probably pass on unless you want to work with that moving forward.

EXPOSURE TO A DIFFERENT ENVIRONMENT

Another assessment that I strongly suggest you make is placing a pup or an adult dog in a new environment. Even if it is simply taking the dog to the front yard or some open area away from the shelter, you want to see how that dog responds to new/different stimuli. Here you're testing for fearfulness. Even though a dog's eyes adjust quickly to light changes, placing a dog in a dark room or in any way altering environmental sounds or other sensory stimulation will also help you assess that dog's confidence.

If you have children, particularly small children, it is good to introduce them into the assessment process as well. While dogs are amazingly adaptable, they will have different initial reactions to children and you could wind up having to deal with an issue down the line.

Another factor to consider is how a dog responds to being in a car. Many of the activities you want to include your dog in involve transporting your dog along with you. Taking a prospective dog for a test ride and assessing his adaptability to that environment will provide useful information. The same is true for crating a dog. Just because a dog is uncomfortable in any of those new environments may not be a reason to eliminate him from consideration, but knowing what you might potentially be getting yourself into is essential to building a bond of trust. Some dogs are curious, some dogs are cautious, and even at the earliest stages of their lives, they will give you some clue to that part of their temperament.

If you aren't able to do those kinds of actual tests in a car or a crate, you can generalize from exposure to a different environment. Any dog who seems overly anxious when exposed to new/different stimuli in one scenario is likely to respond the same way to others.

I make such a strong case for you to be out and actively engaged with your dog in some form of physical movement because those are bonding experiences. Think of the people with whom you are good friends. A lot of the trust and respect that you have for one another was formed because you participated in experiences together. For some humans, that might consist of doing a lot of talking. Since you can't communicate very well that way with your dog, it certainly isn't enough to just chat with him. Doing the things that your dog likes to do isn't the same as letting your dog do whatever he wants. There is an enormous difference between engaging in an activity with your dog and allowing him to exhibit bad manners and poor behavior. I guarantee that if you get out there and be active with your dog, you'll have far fewer violations of manners and conduct to deal with. Think of this as a part of the symbiosis and positive reinforcement. Your dog can come to understand that, by behaving well, he will get the kind of reward that he desires: to be out in the environment.

FOUR

First Steps—Building Trust and Establishing Command and Control

In making my daily rounds at the kennel, I stop at a Belgian Malinois named Carlos. He's lying on his belly, his head resting on his crossed paws. When he sees me, his ears prick up and he rises onto his haunches to sit, expectant. I release the gate and Carlos walks out and stretches, first his front legs and then, a little more gingerly, his back legs. He extends them rearward and I can sense his discomfort. We'll take it easy today, but I know Carlos wants and needs some time with me and some time out of the kennel.

I watch as Carlos trots ahead of me toward the open field where we'll play ball for a bit. I keep my eyes on his hips and notice that in a trot, they're a bit more relaxed, moving with a little bit of side-to-side butt wiggle that is typical for a Belgian Malinois.

Carlos came into my care several years ago. He was seven years old at the time, but he had to retire from the teams. During an operation in Iraq, on a raid that resulted in an intense firefight, he and his handler approached a building suspected of housing cached munitions. Just short of the entryway, a remotely detonated IED threw the pair back several yards. Carlos broke his back and his hind legs and hips and collapsed his sinuses and his lungs. For privacy reasons, I can't go into the injuries his handler sustained other than to say that they were extensive. Medical personnel acted quickly and both the dog and the handler survived.

Carlos nearly prevented that emergency treatment from being initiated. Despite the severity of his injuries, he crawled to his handler's side and took up a defensive perimeter near his fallen comrade. No one trained Carlos to do that. He did it for one reason.

Loyalty.

The two of them had built such a bond that Carlos knew his buddy was hurt, and he wanted to protect him in any way that he could. Carlos recovered sufficiently that he was eventually returned to operational status and served well until he retired at age seven. For a variety of reasons having nothing to do with desire, his handler couldn't bring Carlos into his household, so I was contacted and gladly took the dog in.

I don't want to set off any kind of alarms or stir up a debate, but I'm not a believer that dogs experience emotions in the same way that humans do. This may just be a matter of semantics, but I suppose what I can say is that dogs have a more limited range of emotions and responses and reasons for those responses than we do. Essentially, those responses, reasons, and emotions are just more simple than ours. It's not that they don't exist; they just don't exist to the extent and range of complexity that ours do.

What I also know is that a dog's loyalty to certain human beings (and loyalty isn't an emotion) is impossible to deny. I've seen it. I've experienced it. I admire it. I love it. I work hard to develop it in the relationships that I have with a variety of dogs. That said, it bears repeating that a dog's loyalty is not based on emotion.

In the case of Carlos and his handler, when that dog crawled over to protect that SEAL, he wasn't doing it out of compassion. He didn't feel sorry for a person being wounded. In the animal kingdom, compassion is an exceedingly rare commodity, an anomaly. Carlos wanted to protect that handler, the person whom he had come to rely on for his care and feeding, his play and his work activities. He was loyal to his handler because that man was good to him, that man had proved worthy of Carlos's surrender of leadership to him, had asserted his authority over him.

AN INHERENT TRAIT

In a way, compassion in human beings and loyalty in dogs are parallels. Most people have compassion inherent within them. It is brought out by the people they are surrounded by and the experiences they have. It is not a learned behavior. The same is true with dogs and their loyalty. You can bring loyalty out in dogs, and some of them have it to a greater degree than others, and, like human beings who are sociopaths and lack empathy, some dogs lack loyalty. In my experience those dogs are, thankfully, few and far between.

The reason why we have developed a long and close relationship with the canine species, I believe, is that we each recognize that essential component of our individual natures in one another. Most humans who consider themselves dog lovers do so because they enjoy the companionship, loyalty, intelligence, enthusiasm, and other traits that a dog possesses. We see something of our idealized self in a dog. Dogs can sometimes mirror and reflect our emotions, but more often than not, we project those emotions onto dogs because we want to extend that human/canine connection further.

Does that mean that we should reexamine our relationship with dogs entirely? No. I'm glad that dogs are loyal and, like a lot of you who are reading this book, I appreciate and relish that quality.

The point I want to make is that dogs are *inherently* loyal. As a result, for a lot of reasons, they put up with a lot of crappy behavior from us humans.

The underlying principle of my training philosophy is this:

Dogs possess the capability to be loyal.

As a dog owner you should not take that loyalty for granted or exploit it; you should work to give your dog a reason to be the most loyal to you that he can possibly be.

Be the authority figure that your dog is depending on you to be.

Let your dog know that he can trust you.

BROKEN TRUST

I recently met a dog owner who was frustrated with his relationship with his dog. The man, whom I'll call Bob, was very honest and shared with me the source of the trouble between them. In almost every circumstance, Bob and the dog, whom I'll call Rudy, got along well—except when Bob went into his garage. The two spent a lot of time together doing things around the yard, clearing snow, and raking leaves. Essentially if Bob was outside, Rudy wanted to be out there with him.

Bob was smart enough to figure out what was up with Rudy and the garage. Bob owned a series of cars over the years, older ones that he like to tinker with and fix up and then sell. At one point, when Rudy was about a year and a half old, Bob was trying to remove a rear shock absorber. The nut and bolt were frozen, and no matter what Bob tried, he couldn't get the thing loose. No amount of grunting and applying of force would get that shock off. Bob admitted that he was having a bad day. He was frustrated and angry and started to swear and threw a couple of wrenches around. He noted that Rudy had been in the garage with him at the start, but as he fumed, Rudy was nowhere to be found.

Bob panicked a bit, thinking that Rudy had run off and could possibly be getting into trouble somewhere. The backyard was fenced in but the front was not, and Rudy could have wandered off. That was all Bob needed. Eventually, he found Rudy lying on the floor next to a bed in one of the upstairs bedrooms. When Bob walked in, Rudy eyed him and then looked away. Bob called him, but Rudy didn't respond. Eventually with a little coaxing and a treat or two, Rudy returned to his usual self. That was the last time that Rudy went into the garage with Bob. Since then, he had just flat-out refused, cowering a bit whenever Bob tried to urge him in. Remember that a dog is a simple-association animal. Rudy began to

associate Bob's presence in the garage, his being positioned underneath or somewhere else not inside the car, and the sound of tools
with a lot of shouting and other loud noises. Rudy was stressed by
that commotion, and he didn't want to be stressed. Who does?

Bob was looking to me for ways to get Rudy to break his bad
habit. I had to break the news to Bob that he was the one with the
bad habit. Bob freely admitted that, as much as he loved working on
those old cars, things sometimes went wrong and he got frustrated.
He didn't always throw things or shout, but even if he didn't say
anything, Rudy picked up on his owner's loss of cool. Rudy didn't
want to see that, hear it, or even feel the frustration that came off
Bob. We've probably all been in both Bob's and Rudy's shoes. It can
be really uncomfortable to be around someone who is trying to get a
task done and things just aren't going right. You don't know if your
offering suggestions is a help or a hindrance. You want to tell that
person that whatever is going on is no big deal and that continuing
to work past the point of frustration is just making matters worse.

Rudy couldn't have had any of those thoughts, of course. His
response was far more basic. When Bob lost his cool, even though
Bob didn't direct any of his anger at his dog, Rudy wanted no part of
that scenario. Maybe Rudy was more sensitive to those kinds of
responses than another dog might have been, but Rudy basically lost
respect for Bob. Bob was the guy he expected to be in command and
in control, and he wasn't. What made things worse for Bob was that
he knew that was the case. After having the same scenario repeated,
he eventually made the connection that his outbursts were the cause
of Rudy hightailing it away from him every time Bob went into the
garage and the tools came out. Dogs are very forgiving, and in every

other way, Rudy was right there with Bob. Just not when it came
time to get some work done on the cars.

As problems with a dog go, this is a relatively mild one, but Bob
still felt bad that even though he hadn't had anything like that experience with Rudy for a couple of years, those early outbursts seemed
to have become a permanent fixture in his beloved dog's mind.
Rudy's slinking off to get as far away from Bob as he could was his
way of saying, "I don't trust you right now."

Bob went on to say that he sometimes had problems getting
Rudy to recall (come back to his side) on command. He wondered if
the two circumstances were somehow related. Bob said that he tried
to issue as stern a command as he could, lowering his voice in tone
primarily, but nothing seemed to work. If you put yourself in Rudy's
shoes, then it's no wonder that he sometimes was reluctant to recall
on command. Bob's use of a different voice likely sounded like the
one Rudy associated with anger and frustration. Would you want to
be alongside someone who sounds angry and annoyed?

I cite this example mainly to show how trust can be broken. It
may not change the nature of the relationship entirely, but there are
consequences. In many ways, trust is like a sheet of paper. If you
crumple up that paper, you can smooth it out again. It will never be
exactly the same, but that doesn't mean you have to discard it either.

Other circumstances besides a dog's perception of negative emotions can alter a relationship. An overeager greeting, as I mentioned
earlier, can also make a dog less likely to trust you. I'm not suggesting that every time you encounter a dog you have to be super serious, but only over time and after the bond of trust has been built
would it be appropriate to behave that way. You shouldn't interpret a

dog's showing a lot of immediate affection toward you as trust; some dogs, like some people, like a lot of attention and affection. That doesn't mean they necessarily trust you.

IN COMMAND OF YOURSELF AND IN CONTROL OF YOUR DOG

We've gone over command and control in many situations. But to train your dog the Navy SEAL way, you must demonstrate an ability to remain calm, keep your focus directed on the task at hand, and be forceful in communicating your expectations. If you show your dog that you're unflappable and you consistently project an image of authority, then your dog will understand that he can count on you. Your dog will recognize that instantly and will be far more likely to behave in the ways that you want and learn to do the kinds of things you want.

Some people have the ability to command a room or a situation. They have that "it factor" that lets you know that they are in control. If you don't believe that you're that type of person, when it comes to training your dog, you should at least be able to conjure an image in mind of someone who is extremely self-possessed. Think of a time when you felt most in control. Maybe it was a time you delivered a speech in a class or a presentation at work. Maybe it was a time that you had to discipline one of your kids. Maybe it was when you stood your ground in dealing with a threatening stranger who posed a potential threat.

If you've ever been around a litter of puppies and their mother, you can keep that image in mind. A mother rarely plays with her young. She understands that her role is to be guardian. She protects her pups, teaches them, and serves as an example for how they should behave.

I'd like you to try this experiment if possible. Go to a public place where dogs and owners have congregated, preferably one where dogs are off leash and can interact with you at will. When a dog approaches you, keep your hands in your pockets, maintain your full height, and glance at the dog briefly while maintaining an indifferent attitude. If he shows interest in you, then respond in a cordial manner, just as you would in meeting any new person.

What you are looking for is how the dog responds to you. You are putting the ball, so to speak, in the dog's court. Instead of being forward and trying to "meet" him, let the dog show you who he is. Based on the dog's response to you, you'll be able to see if he is shy (he ignores you); if he is friendly and curious (he comes up to you); if he is too energetic and needy (he jumps at you and works hard to get your attention and affection); or if he is fearful (he backs off or shows signs of defensiveness—raised hackles, baring of teeth, barking, growling).

The key thing to remember, as is true later on in training, is to make the dog offer the behavior and don't try to elicit a reaction—be in command of yourself and evaluate the dog.

A DOG'S PERSPECTIVE

I often use the following analogy when working with handlers of MWDs and other people who are interested in learning about training dogs. Imagine a scenario in which you are placed in a ten-foot-by-ten-foot prison cell with another person. You're in a foreign country where you don't speak the language and it is clear this other person is from that country. How are you going to act? How are you going to get that person to respect you and not take advantage of you in any way?

You don't want to appear threatening, but you also don't want to appear too submissive. That firm middle ground between those two poles is where you have to be, particularly when first working with an unfamiliar dog. Puppies are at a lower developmental level, so they may not understand the signals that you're sending. At some point in that encounter, you may offer to share resources with that other individual as a way to let them know that you're a good person. You're willing to offer them something—not as a way to keep them from taking what you have, but as an opportunity to show that you are operating from a position of power or abundance. They will derive some benefit from being cooperative with you.

FIRST THINGS FIRST

Working with your dog the Navy SEAL way means that you will approach what most people commonly lump together in the same category as "training" into two elements. The first phase that I work on is developing the dog's respect for me, his manners, and his sense of boundaries. For every dog owner those last two are going to vary somewhat—what you might deem acceptable conduct I may not, and vice versa.

These first three elements—respect, manners, and boundaries—are all interrelated. A dog who respects your authority won't jump on you, for example. House-training your dog is an example of a sense of boundaries—*this is where I am to do this*. Boundaries also have to do with what parts of the house you allow the dog to be in, what objects he is allowed to put in his mouth, where he is allowed to be rambunctious and play. Again, you set the limits and make those determinations.

From the beginning, I suggest that ball playing and other forms of higher-energy play be done outside the home. Teach that basic principle—inside is for calm and outside is for energetic—from the earliest days with your dog and you will have fewer problems down the line. Your dog will understand that boundary very quickly. If you decide that a basement, a family room, or some other area of the house is also an acceptable place for play and displays of energy, that's fine. Just be consistent in enforcing those boundaries.

It's also important at this stage, and even later on, to limit the number of objects that you use as play toys. Many people have complained to me about destructive dogs who chew up their belongings. In many cases, I've seen those homes and how they are littered with dog toys along with their own possessions. How is the dog going to learn to differentiate "mine" from "theirs" in that case?

In terms of manners, I employ much the same standards that I do in teaching my children about human-to-human interactions. You respect other people's sense of space and their property and belongings, and you have a sense of decorum about the level of noise and distraction that you create that is different depending on the environment you are in—again, the inside and outside distinction.

You will primarily rely on your body language to communicate your expectations to your dog during this phase.

Think of the earliest days of your education. You learned to sit still, be quiet, and have control over when you spoke out loud before you had any kind of formal classroom instruction about your ABCs, numbers, or any other subject information. You had to be in the right frame of mind and behavior for learning before you could be taught other concepts. It's all part of being educated. But any teacher will tell you that if they do not have respect from and authority over their students, very little if any learning can take place. The same is true with training a dog.

With an older dog, addressing respect, manners, and boundaries first is even more essential. He has lived in and adapted to (or not adapted to) a set of expectations. You have to make it clear immediately that a new set of demands is going to be placed on him.

Again, you have to use your situational awareness and decide from what baseline you are working. If you have an older dog who has already demonstrated respect, proper manners, and a sense of appropriate boundaries, you can move on to training immediately.

FIRST CONTACT

A dog's first day in your home is, in most cases, not the time to lay down the law to show that you're the hardass in charge. Again, you want your dog's experience with you to be a positive one. But that also doesn't mean that when you first bring the dog home, you lie on the ground and let him climb all over you, spread around a bunch of toys and balls, and generally go nuts with him.

What I do with a "new" dog is find as neutral an environment as possible and simply spend time with him. I'll sit in a small uncluttered room, a backyard empty of other people or dogs or other distractions, or a garage alone with that dog. Not only should the environment be neutral, so should your emotional state and your body language. Being indifferent is not a bad thing in these early stages. Simply let the dog investigate the area. Just being with you, not making any demands on him, you're building the early stages of the bond that will evolve into trust.

I know that some people are uncomfortable with the idea of indifference. Of course you should be excited about having a new dog in your house. Of course the experience should be pleasurable. But here's where keeping that big-picture/long-term outlook has to come into play. If you take the time to build the proper trusting relationship, keep your emotions at bay, remain in control as the authority, and work to garner the dog's respect rather than admiration, then you'll have years and years of a high-quality and loving relationship. If you don't do those things, you could have months, if not years, of frustrations as the two of you work through issues that have their roots in those earliest days together. Another benefit to playing this properly is that your dog will never resent you for not paying him enough attention.

Time is your best friend in developing your human/canine relationship into one where you are best friends. Keep that "new" dog around you as you work around or inside the house. Simply being with the dog in those early stages, and being a calm presence in the middle of all the new stimuli that the dog is experiencing after being separated from what he's known before, will be enough. Look at this situation from your dog's perspective, imagine what it would be like for you to be transported to a new environment with new people, and I think you'll better understand why a neutral and low-key approach is best.

That said, if a dog doesn't have any respect for you, doesn't have a sense of manners, and doesn't understand boundaries at all, you will have to be even more assertive, more fully develop your in-command persona, and take immediate steps to get that dog under control.

PROVIDE A NEUTRAL SPACE

Crate training is an effective tool for providing your dog with a neutral space. The reason I call it a neutral space is that it is an area where your dog can't get into any kind of trouble. I recommend using a crate for both puppies and older dogs first being brought into the house. Place it in a central area of the home where the dog will be able to see everyone and observe the interactions and goings-on in the household. Frequently take the dog out of the crate for playtime, housebreaking, and feeding. Return the dog to the crate after these brief sessions.

While I call it a neutral space, you should still work toward creating positive associations. Make the crate as comfortable as possible for the dog. Don't use it as an area for the dog version of time-outs. You can still interact with the dog while he's in there—obviously in a more limited way—as well as providing toys as a form of stimulation.

Using a crate reinforces another important concept in your dog's mind. It lets him know that you are in control of another large part of his life—his ability to be outside and interacting with his environment. Just as you control his food and water intake and other aspects of his life, he should look to you as the person who gives him the opportunity to do the things that he most enjoys doing—being active.

ONE LEADER

Even before you bring a new dog into your home, it's important to establish who is going to be primarily responsible for care and training. Your dog needs a team leader, and you will only confuse him if he has to figure out the dynamics of multiple relationships and how the hierarchy works. Just as in raising kids, it's important for both parents to come to some agreement about various approaches; you and any partner(s) you have in living with that dog have to do the same thing. A set of clear expectations helps, and I know that in the real world that isn't always executed. I'll get to some of the issues related to mixed messages and mixed expectations later in the book.

For now, understand that one person has to be the team leader. That person is also responsible for making it clear to the dog that his or her expectations as team leader apply across the board. Even when that team leader isn't present, the same sets of expectations and consequences have to be in place. That goes for the other humans in the relationship as well. That said, it all stems from the team leader. Take, for example, a no-begging-at-the-table expectation. As the team leader, you can't sit at your place at the table and expect your five-year-old to manage a situation where the dog is pestering for food. In theory it's a good idea to have your child be responsible for enforcing that expectation, but if the dog is engaging in that bad behavior, he's doing it because he perceives a vacuum in leadership. That means that you as team leader have to intervene and more clearly demonstrate that there are consequences for not meeting your expectation.

"PARENTING" A DOG

I also ask people to think about how they interact with their children and what tone they have set from the beginning in terms of authority and control. I parent my children in much the same way my father did. First and foremost, my kids understand that I am their father. I'm the one who has authority over them. This is my house. You live here thanks to me and I set the rules around here. Eventually, they'll see other sides of our relationship and I can roll around the floor and have fun with them, but when I give them the look that says enough is enough and I'm now back in the role as their father, they get it and they fall in line and respond to me accordingly.

Likewise, you want your dog to understand that this is a positive relationship. All good things that he wants and needs flow through you. Whether you are working with a puppy or a more mature dog, the person who will be responsible for the dog's training should be the one who feeds the dog, provides water, allows the dog out to relieve himself, takes him outside to play, and understands and responds to his primary motivation. For home training done by nonprofessionals, the earliest stages of training need to be done by one person. You can try to do team teaching, but you're most likely going to end up confusing the dog and prolonging the most basic training.

Once the dog has mastered the basic commands, has his manners in place, and understands his boundaries, then the team leader can integrate others into the training of the dog. Depending on the circumstances, this may mean that the team leader is solely responsible for the dog for a few weeks to a few months.

What Is It Going to Take?
What Am I Going to Get?

For most dogs that primary motivation will be one of three things, and most likely a combination thereof:

Food

Play

Affection

Before you begin any kind of training, you have to understand what your dog likes. Not only do you have to give your dog a reason to trust you, but you also have to give him a reason to do the things you're expecting him to do. Don't assume that what you think your dog wants is an accurate assessment of what his primary motivation is. Don't just settle for paying out what you're willing to give, but really assess that dog's motivation.

Think of it like this: If you are forced to work and receive no salary or benefits, how likely are you to bust your ass and perform at your highest level? Unless you're some kind of masochist, you're going to work your hardest and your best for someone you respect, not someone you fear or someone who you simply like but don't respect.

There is a big difference between liking the work you do for someone and liking the person for whom you work. I can tell you that, in teams, there were people in charge of me whom I didn't necessarily like as individuals or want to pal around with, but I did like working for them. Why? Because I respected and trusted them, and they respected and trusted me. Certainly it is much better to also like that individual, but it took more time to develop that kind of more complicated relationship. Things always work out better if the respect comes first and the friendship comes later. The same is true with your relationship with your dog.

REWARDS AS A TEACHER

If you establish from the beginning that when your dog does what you want, he gets some kind of reward, then you've taken the first major step necessary to get your dog to do most anything you want him to do. The thing to keep in mind about all aspects of training, whether it is basic obedience, tricks and stunts, search and rescue, or detection and apprehension, is that one irrefutable fact underlies your dog's behavior:

When a behavior is consistently rewarded, it is most likely to occur again.

As a result, you have to become incredibly self-aware and situationally aware to make sure that you are rewarding the right things. You have to reward with conscious and precise intention. If you have kids, you know that the foundational statement about rewards and repetition is true. If your child is in a high chair eating and tosses something onto the floor and you smile or laugh or make some kind of sound that indicates pleasure, he is damn sure going to repeat that behavior. Even if you think you were looking stern and discouraging that kind of behavior, you have to be absolutely sure that you are acting out your desired intent. That is even more important with dogs. Kids can pick up on a lot of unintended nonverbal cues, but dogs, as we've already established, rely almost entirely on nonverbal cues. An unintended reward is still a reward.

It is equally important to reward a dog for doing a good thing even if you haven't expressly made a demand for it. Let's say you've worked with your dog to go to his bed or some other area of the house after greeting company. Reward the dog by going over to him and offering a few simple words of praise. More important, get down on his level, pet him, and spend a few seconds with him. I'm frequently surprised by how seldom some owners interact with their dogs on the dog's level—not acting like a dog, but physically moving into the space the dog occupies. Once you have a good relationship with that dog, doing so is a reward. Not doing so is a way to send a negative signal. Dogs are highly social creatures who live in groups. When you make the move to join a dog, to form a small group, you're tying into his elementary nature and needs. There is an enormous difference between rewarding your dog with attention or affection when he approaches you and when you approach him.

Notice the difference between how your dog responds in terms of behavior and body language when either you or he takes the lead in establishing contact. Think about what a difference it makes in your day if your boss approaches you to tell you that you've done good work.

It is important to send negative signals as well as positive ones. Just as never rewarding a dog is a bad idea, so are unending rewards. Dogs need some context in order to understand what is acceptable and what is not. Without context, a reward becomes meaningless. It becomes what is expected and the norm. In order for your dog to understand that some behavior and reward is good, he also has to understand the converse.

The inverse of that first statement about rewards and repetition is also true:

Whatever behavior isn't rewarded will be extinguished.

You also have to keep this in mind. I've been in many households with dogs, and often the overwhelming percentage of interactions between the people and the dog is negative. That means that few rewards are presented for the dog who is doing something expected of him. And worse, what attention the dog does get is negative—a reprimand for some misbehavior.

Let me add another concept to these basic principles.

Whatever behavior is consistently rewarded will be repeated.

Whatever behavior consistently is not rewarded will be extinguished.

It may seem too obvious to state, but consistency is essential. Sending a mixed signal will do exactly that—mix him up.

That also applies to how you deliver a reward or a correction. As I mentioned, getting down to your dog's level and petting him is a strong reward. While working through a training scenario, going down to a knee to give a dog a treat uses body language as a signal to reinforce the positive. If you do this while correcting or denying a reward in some way, you've lessened the impact of the association you're trying to create. Your dog is thinking:

On my level (reduction in height differential) = I've done a good thing.

BODY LANGUAGE AND CORRECTION

Keep that body language message clear. Whenever you correct a dog, keep your shoulders back, your head and body square to the dog, your feet spread—the most empowered stance you can deliver. If you don't go down to one knee to praise or reward, you should at least soften your body position. The same is true of the distance you keep between yourself and the dog.

Your dog will pick up on these subtle cues.

Using your body to close the distance toward the dog to highlight your intent even further.

Slower and relaxed movement + close, friendly contact = good dog.

Commanding movement + no friendly contact = bad dog.

You need to use your body to regulate behavior that is taking place. Your reaction and your intent have to match what your body is doing. For example, if you don't like it when your dog rushes to the door and barks whenever there's a knock or the bell rings, you have to put yourself between the door and the dog, using a knee or your hips to put him in the location you want him to be. At the same time, your voice has to be commanding, not shouting and screaming, but a stern "No," or some other strong sound. Remember, your dog doesn't understand words the way we do. He understands the sounds, the pitch, and the volume.

How do you reward the dog when he places himself, at your urging, in the location you want? Simply backing away from him and releasing the pressure you've placed on his body is a reward. You've ended that confrontation. Supplementing that with a reward will help reinforce the point.

If you try to use your body to block your dog and don't get him moving where you want him to be, don't give up. Giving up is rewarding him for resisting your efforts. If he wins that battle and gets what he wants—to be at the door—then the more times he wins, the more difficult it will be to extinguish that behavior down the line.

NOT ALL REWARDS ARE EQUAL

Dog trainers use the term *flooding* to describe the top end of a sliding scale of administering rewards. The idea is simple. For basic obedience or performance, provide a small reward. For more complicated behaviors or to encourage more highly desirable behaviors, amp up the rewards by presenting them in succession. For example, in working with our more advanced explosives-detection dogs, we sometimes have them discover a small trace of a compound in a kiddie pool filled with plastic bottles. That's a relatively easy find for a dog. They get one toss of a ball and a quick reinforcement reward for a job well done. Later, we work a detection scenario in which the dog has to cover a lot of ground, investigate several buildings and various other possible hiding sites, and so on. When he makes the find and then alerts us to his success with a specific behavior to let us know he's got it, then we provide sustained reward, lavish praise, repeated ball fetching, and so on. It is possible to reward a dog too much, to truly flood him to a point of complete saturation at which the reward loses its meaning. Rewards, like corrections, should be proportional. The surest way to reduce the effectiveness of a reward is to overuse it.

Here's a quick review of the most essential concepts to consider as you make the first initial steps toward training:

- Give your dog a reason to be loyal to you.
- Be the authority figure that your dog is depending on you to be.
- Let your dog know that he can trust you.
- Broken trust can be repaired.
- You have to be in command and in control.
- Neutral first contact helps build trust down the line.
- A single team leader initially is best, but everyone needs to be in agreement and involved.
- Identify whether food, play, or affection/attention is your dog's primary motivator.
- Whatever behavior is rewarded gets repeated.
- Whatever behavior is unrewarded or punished gets extinguished.
- Consistent application of rewards and consequences is essential.
- Use body language as a primary source of correction.
- Not all rewards are equal.

Proper position for your dog when implementing the "stay" command.

After the dog has performed a correct stay, he should recall directly back to you just like this.

If you can master these simple concepts and take control of your demeanor, the rest is easy in comparison.

STAY?

Some trainers believe that it isn't necessary to teach a dog to stay. They believe that "stay" is an inherent part of sitting or downing. While that's true, and I understand the continuing rationale that once you have taught a dog to sit or "down," you should be able to walk away and have that dog remain fixed in that position, I still teach "stay."

I believe it's important for a dog to understand the associations of that behavior separate from any other commands. That way, no matter what his body position is—sitting, downing, standing, or moving—I have a way to get him to remain in a location, regardless.

"Stay" along with "recall" or "come" or "here" are the most important because they involve your dog's safety and potentially the safety of others. These concepts need to be absolutes in the repertoire of a well-behaved and well-trained dog.

FIVE

Basic Training Principles

find it funny that of all the questions I get asked about the military working dogs that I've provided for various special operations forces, the one that I hear most often is: How did you train those dogs to run on a treadmill? Maybe because most civilians can relate to that device—they may have used it themselves—they can relate to it in some personal way. I think they'd be interested in how we trained them to do the clearing operations the dogs participated in or got them accustomed to the helicopters they flew in or the harnesses they wore when fast-roping or parachuting out of aircraft. No, it is the treadmill that most fascinates people.

The training methods and the principles that I use to get those dogs to do some pretty extraordinary things are the same ones that you can do with your dog to get him to do ordinary things. All of the principles that I summarized at the end of the last chapter are important, of course, but you need a few more practical pieces of the puzzle to complete the picture of an obedient and well-trained dog.

The first is that you have to use your multiple-perspective focus and have a vision of the end product you want to attain. That means that you have to envision how you want your dog to behave in terms of (1) control—heeling, sitting, downing, recalling, staying—and then (2) what I touched on briefly before in terms of respect, manners, and boundaries.

It is important to have a plan along with a vision. How and when you are going to conduct those training sessions, how your dog's nontraining time is going to be structured, and what kind of control you're going to have over your dog when you're not actively engaged in training all need to be accounted for.

At what age and how intensely can you begin to work on control? As soon as you bring a pup home, you can begin his "formal" training. Young puppies have the attention span of a very young child, so those sessions should be very short, no more than a few minutes, five to ten times a day. More than anything else, these sessions are going to be about relationship building and trust. They should be entirely positive for you and the dog and should seem more like fun than anything else.

Even in these earliest days, you're communicating to your dog that there is a time and a place for his training. That means having one area set aside where it is one person and the dog alone. Your dog will begin to associate that place with an area where a certain set of behaviors and expectations exist. You have treats that you use as a reward. Your dog will know when you have them and when you don't and will begin to associate the smell, the sight, and the presentation of those treats with specific behaviors.

From your dog's perspective it works like this:

We go to this place. → My team leader has treats with him in that place. → When we go to that place and my team leader has treats with him, I get them when I do X.

These short sessions of several minutes or so, which should end on a positive note when the dog has been able to offer a desirable behavior a few times before he becomes too distracted, will suffice in the earliest stages. Sometimes it may take longer and that's okay. When you see that you're headed toward a point of diminishing returns or the dog is distracted or is on the verge of losing attention completely, stop the session. After a break of a few minutes, you can resume. These extended sessions should occur rarely because even if the dog lies down, goes near his crate, sits, or does anything that you eventually want the dog to do or is a part of a desired behavior, you will be rewarding that dog. Success can, and often does, come in very small increments. If you try to wait for a dog to offer a "complete" behavior before a reward, you'll likely go a long time before issuing that reward.

If those first few minutes were successful, end the session. To do that, play with the dog a bit, let him freely be a dog, or put him in his crate or return him to wherever he has been spending most of his time. Returning the dog to his neutral zone signals the end of that session.

Teaching dogs about a purposeful time in a specific place as a part of their daily routine is as important as it is for schools to have bells and teachers to let kids know that class is now in session and class is now over. Using that same analogy, having a training space is like having a classroom. That environment signals to the dog that this is a place he goes where he is required to meet a certain set of expectations.

How long will it take for a dog to get the message about the location and the expectations there? It all depends on the dog. If you conduct yourself with the kind of purposeful intent and seriousness necessary, you'll go a long way toward speeding up the process of understanding. This is the first phase of the learning process. Once your dog is overwhelmingly successful in completing the tasks assigned, you'll move outside the classroom to see how he will manage with increasing levels of distraction. You'll move back and forth between the classroom and outside it as you teach new behaviors.

Just like students in a classroom, we need our dogs to focus on the teacher.

While I suggest two- to three-minute sessions initially, that's not a completely ironclad rule. Depending on what you're trying to teach, how taxing the performance of that behavior seems to be, and how successful your dog is being in offering the desired behavior, that time could either expand or collapse from session to session. Essentially, the burden is on you to be able to read your dog. I will caution you against this: Don't get too far ahead of yourself and your dog. For example, after only a few repetitions of successful sitting, don't move immediately to downing.

Be patient.

Rushing through things now will only lead to issues and more time spent down the road. Multiple repetitions and multiple reinforcements will cement the association in your dog's brain.

OFFERING VS. ORDERING

Old-school training methods relied primarily on forcing a dog to do something. Want him to sit? Push his rear end down. Want him to lie down? Use a leash to drag his neck and chest to the floor.

Would you want to learn like that? That would be similar to someone setting you down in front of a math worksheet and pressing your head to it, hoping that somehow you'd understand long division. Eventually you might figure it out, but you really wouldn't enjoy the experience or want to do long division at every opportunity.

The main reason why I can't say how long it will take to get your dog to perform one of the basic training behaviors consistently is because instead of forcing a behavior to occur, you are waiting for it to be willingly and consistently performed and then rewarding it.

This is where your patience comes in. You walk into that initial training session with a plan in mind. Today we are going to work on sitting. You have your treats, you have your clicker (more on that in a moment), and you assume your neutral/authoritative stance. Only when your dog offers that behavior—he sits—do you offer the reward to reinforce the behavior.

Offering versus forcing a behavior makes a huge difference in how your dog learns. It may sound like a bit of a guessing game, but the kind of mental stimulation that goes on when your dog figures out what he has to do to get the reward creates a series of links in his brain that no amount of butt-pushing or other physical contact can do. I'm not going to get into how neurons fire in the brain and what chemical processes take place in the cells to get neurons to join together and so on. Just know this: When you learn something and you figure it out for yourself through a series of connections, it stays with you longer than a simple one-off. For example, think of anything relatively complex that you know how to do—typing, for example. If I asked you to recite the letters on the top row of the keyboard, that would probably be more difficult for you than simply typing a sentence I presented to you. Your brain and your body working together make it easier to remember the location of those letters outside the context of a practical application. It is easier to remember by doing and thinking than it is by just thinking.

That's true for your dog and his offering of a behavior.

In those early control-training sessions, continue to offer a treat to your dog as a reward for sitting. I don't believe that a vocalization or a gesture is necessary at this point to pair with that offered behavior. I've done this numerous times with people who absolutely believe that their dog knows the meaning of the word *sit*. I accept their challenge. I call the dog over, and when that dog approaches me, I say "Broccoli" and the dog sits.

Why?

Mostly because the string of associations that dog has is contextual and not verbal. That dog understands that in a situation in which a human calls him over, pauses, and then emits some sound, he's expected to sit. You probably understand that "command" words don't really have the same meaning for you as they do for your dog. You could, as I did, make any kind of vocalization and associate it in your dog's mind with any behavior. So why have that clutter? It would make sense to have those words if that were the only way you had available to communicate your desires to your dog.

When you speak, you rarely make a nondescript utterance without some nonverbal component—intonation and physical gestures mostly. You may think that your dog is responding to the word *sit*, but he is more likely doing what you ask in response to the inflected tone of your words and some movement of your body.

Few people have the kinesthetic (movement) intelligence to be fully aware all the time of what every part of their body is doing at any given instant. When you say the word *sit* you are likely nodding your head, bowing forward slightly at the waist, bending your knees, or some combination of all those things, along with moving your facial muscles in a particular way. You may not intentionally be performing those movements, but your dog is picking up on them.

"CLICK" MARKS THE SPOT

Along with patience and proper use of body language (as opposed to verbal commands), learning how to *mark* your dog's behavior is essential to the training methodology the Navy SEAL way. By marking a behavior you are in a sense taking a snapshot or photo of the desired behavior. I've had great success using a handheld clicker as a noise-making device to alert the dog being trained at the precise moment he has performed the desired action. This clicker serves as a *bridge* or a *conditioned reinforcer*. I like the term *bridge* because it helps you better understand how the device works as a training aid. For example, if you are working on "sit," and you have the clicker in your hand, as soon as your dog puts his butt on the ground, you activate it. Next you immediately provide the reward.

A BRIEF HISTORY OF CLICKER TRAINING

Two graduate students of the psychologist B. F. Skinner, Marian Kruse and Keller Breland, developed the idea of using a marker as part of operant conditioning. They did their work during World War II. Later, they formed a company called Animal Behavior Enterprises (ABE). Later, Bob Bailey joined them. He was the U.S. Navy's first director of animal training.

ABE did some amazing work with all kinds of animals. For the CIA, they trained cats to navigate through city streets and into buildings, carrying radios. They trained dolphins to locate targets at a great distance from their handlers. They also trained birds, guided by a laser, to fly to specific locations on a building to allow the cameras strapped to them to spy on the individuals inside.

Karen Pryor was an early advocate for clicker training. She saw how large marine mammals were being trained through the use of whistles as the marking device. She credits a number of other trainers for helping to spread the word in the mid- to late 1990s. Since then, clicker training has become a more accepted method.

Though it's impossible to come up with an accurate number of how many dogs have been clicker trained, do a quick online search using the term *clicker training* and you will see just how prevalent it has become.

The sequence goes like this:

Desired behavior → click → reward

Earlier, I used the word *snapshot*. Think of the clicker's sound being like a camera's shutter. Your dog hears that sound and associates it with the behavior that immediately preceded it. The actual reward is what will cement that association. Also, the click itself is a way of saying to the dog that he just did what was desired.

Timing is everything here. You have likely seen dogs who move from one behavior to another quickly in order to earn a reward. As a result, a quick trigger finger helps to separate the desired behavior from others being offered. Here's when command of your body language also enters the picture—or maybe I should say exits. You want the dog to associate the sound of the clicker with his behavior and the reinforcement. To do that, you must keep your body language as neutral as possible. Also, since you used your body as a correction before to establish your authority and your dog has the proper understanding of where he fits in the hierarchy, you want this training to be completely free of any associations with your perhaps having to intimidate him in some way. This is now all about behaviors and reinforcement of those desired behaviors.

I previously mentioned Karen Pryor as having a great deal of influence on my thinking about dogs. While she is certainly not the first person to employ marker training, she is probably the most responsible for introducing it on a large scale to broad-spectrum dog training. In a 1997 speech at the Association for Behavior Analysis conference, she wisely pointed out that behaviors that sometimes took months and even years for an animal to master could sometimes be accomplished in days or weeks with clicker training. By pinpointing and communicating exactly what you expect the animal to do, you eliminate a lot of the confusion that slows the process.

She also believes that the sound of the click and the clicker itself become a reward. The click sets up a sense of anticipation in the dog, an "I'm going to get something!" moment, and then the reward comes. Think about your own experiences and how the smell of your favorite meal cooking is a pleasurable experience. An entire ad campaign for a brand of ketchup was based on the idea of anticipation and how those moments before the taste were almost enough. I've seen myself how doubling the reward can work to speed the training process.

GETTING STARTED WITH THE CLICKER

A clicker is a small handheld device that makes a clicking sound when pressed. A number of manufacturers produce them; some of them have raised and others recessed buttons, some emit a louder sound, and they vary in price from a few dollars to ten or more. Their essential function is the same—they make a noise that is loud enough for your dog to hear. You could snap your fingers or make some other sound yourself, but the clicker both is distinct and allows you to make that sound with great timing precision and consistency. A quick Internet search will yield dozens of results for various types of clickers.

Before you use the clicker with any behavioral training, you have to *load* or *charge* the clicker. That means you have to help the dog make the association between the specific sound of the clicker and his getting a reward. Do this ten to twelve times in the period of a couple of minutes. Click. Reward. Pause. Click. Reward.

It is also important that you not show the dog the reward before he offers a behavior or before you press the clicker during the loading phase. Otherwise, down the line your dog may not perform some of the behaviors you require unless treats are present. The way to combat that is to use more than one type of reward—in other words, don't use food as a reward all the time. You'll notice that I use

Tools of the trade: a good collapsible treat pouch and a clicker to reinforce desired behaviors.

the term *reward* throughout this section. A reward doesn't, and shouldn't, always mean food.

It may take your dog several sessions with the clicker to make the positive association.

After you've accomplished that task and the dog has demonstrated his understanding by showing some anticipation and attention to indicate that the clicker has come to mean a future reward, move on to using the clicker with any behavior. Over time, the mere sight of the clicker device may set your dog's anticipation in motion. Seeing you reach into your pocket or seeing the device will help establish the mind-set that training and rewards are in the dog's future. However, it is the sound that the clicker makes that marks the desired behaviors and really cements the association in the dog's mind. If the dog becomes too excitable or is too fixated on the appearance of the device itself, you will have to desensitize him to the sight of the device.

To do that, keep the clicker out of view. They are small enough to fit in your hand. (That said, some dogs may be able to identify them by scent.) So you can either hide the clicker or otherwise disguise it. Don't reward the dog for responding to the sight of the clicker by offering up desired behaviors without the sound having been made to mark the behavior. To desensitize the dog to the sight of the clicker, you may have to have several sessions where you have a clicker out and present but don't use the clicker to mark any behaviors.

Many trainers use what is called *shaping* when working with dogs. That means clicking and rewarding something that approximates the desired behavior or is one small part of a more complex behavior. For example, if you are working on "heel" and your dog comes to you and stands alongside you but is not facing forward, begin by rewarding his proximity to you and then continue to click and reward as he gets closer and closer to the whole behavior being correct.

TRAINING THE HANDLERS

I often use a role-playing game to help people master their clicking skills. I have an electronic collar and a pair of individuals. One person plays the role of the dog and the other plays the handler. I place an assortment of items on a table, much like what you might have in your junk drawer in your kitchen. The "dog" sits down at the table and the handler places the e-collar around the upper arm of the person he is trying to train. The collar is uncomfortable enough that by itself it is a positive punishment for the person acting as a dog.

I then take the handler out of the room and say to him, for example, "I want you to train that dog to take the little green army man and then place a rubber band around its head and then take the four dice and place them in a square around the rubber-banded army man. You can't communicate at all with that dog verbally."

I give the handler the remote for the e-collar and he returns to the room. They both sit there. As soon as the "dog" touches one of the items, unless it's the army man or one of the involved objects, he gets a mild shock. Very soon, the "dog" will stop touching anything on the table. Later, we remove the collar and use the clicker/reward. I assign another task to be completed with a few of the items. The "dog" gets a click and then a gummy bear or some other kind of treat when he touches the correct item. In some cases, I don't use the food reward at all—the absence of the shock is enough of a reward.

Not one person has ever completed this task correctly when shock is involved. Almost every time with the click/reward, the "dog" completes it within five to ten minutes. That's how effective clicker training is. It has been used with all kinds of animals and even humans and really speeds learning. More than that, it is fun. When I do this demonstration and shock is in play, the subjects both sit there looking downcast with their shoulders slumped and nervous expressions on their faces. In contrast, when it's clicker time, the handlers are laughing and enjoying themselves, moving to touch as many objects as quickly as possible to solve the puzzle and earn the reward.

ADDING THE COMMAND WORD

You don't want to lump too many associations together too early. For that reason, to this point, you aren't saying anything or signaling the dog to take a particular action. Wait until your dog has demonstrated his ability to offer a particular behavior reliably enough that you can predict when he's about to do it before using a command word or gesture. Be aware that your dog has no concept of what words mean. In other words, if you repeatedly say the word *down*, as in "down, down, down," your dog will associate that more lengthy expression as his cue to lie down. Keep it simple and clear.

When you add verbal commands, you will continue to click and reward as before, but now you will reward the dog only for doing the action in response to that specific word. Ignore any spontaneous offerings of the behavior. When you first stop giving a reward for any offering of the behavior, expect that your dog will start to offer it to you more and more. Put yourself in your dog's perspective again: "For a while, every time I performed this action I got a reward." What would you be likely to do? You'd be like the person at the computer that has frozen and you'd keep hitting that escape key or clicking that mouse button hoping for the same result that has worked in the past. Experts call this influx of behavioral offerings an *extinction burst*. If you consistently ignore the uncued offering of a behavior, it will eventually stop. If it doesn't, then you have some work to do and you will need to go back to the earliest phase of clicking and rewarding that behavior.

THE CORRECT CORRECTION

Corrections are part of operant conditioning. They can be either positive punishments (adding something) or negative punishments (taking something away). In either case, they are used to teach the difference between undesirable and desirable behaviors.

Consequently, not only does the correction have to fit the crime, it has to suit the dog. For some dogs, particularly shy ones, a harsh-sounding verbal correction can be too strong. It will instill fear, which is not respect. For other dogs, a verbal correction, no matter how harsh the sounds or how loudly those sounds are delivered, may not always be enough.

Sometimes, depending on the context, you will have to use a combination of a verbal and a physical correction. How stout a tug on the dog's collar or how stern the sounds have to be depends on the dog. Also, some people, no matter how hard they try, may not be able to produce a vocalization that sounds very stern. That's okay. It's all a question of context. If you use one tone for praise, a similar tone for general commands, and a different one for a correction, your dog will differentiate among them. The key then is to develop a distinct sound quality for each.

THE "PLACE" COMMAND

With my dogs, the first control behavior I work on is *placing*. I prefer to use an elevated dog bed for this training exercise. An elevated bed is exactly what you might think—a raised and cushioned platform on four legs. I set that dog bed in the middle of the training area and then stand about ten feet away from it. I assume my customary neutral authoritative stance. As with any basic training scenario, I wait for the dog to offer the behavior. I want that dog to get

A perfect execution of the first behavior, the "place" command, on an elevated dog bed.

on that elevated bed and then stay there, either sitting or lying down. I feel fortunate if I can get a dog to offer that complete behavior within a day or several short sessions. Sometimes it may take longer, but in my mind it is worth every second it takes to do this as the initial behavior I reinforce before moving on to any others. If you don't have an elevated bed, a crate or any other specific location or object you want the dog to go to and lie down on will also suffice.

As you might expect, I click and reward incrementally as the dog proceeds. First, if he looks toward that bed, I click and reward. If he takes a step toward it, click and reward. If he gets near the bed and sniffs it or shows any kind of interest in it, click and reward. If he makes a move toward putting his paws on the bed, click and reward. As I mentioned before, once he completes the behavior I reward more heavily.

Incrementally rewarding is the only way you will get to the end goal. You have to reward the dog for taking those baby steps. It is rare for a dog to offer you the full behavior immediately, or at least with any real consistency. The dog focuses his attention on me, but my resuming my neutral attitude after rewarding sends a signal to the dog that he's going to have to do something else to earn another one. People often make the mistake of luring the dog, baiting the dog, or otherwise trying to get the dog to perform the behavior instead of waiting for the dog to offer it. Remain neutral in posture and in attitude and in so doing teach the dog that he has to go away from you and try other alternatives on his own in order to get the click and reward.

If you cue your dog, then he will remain focused on your actions and not offer other behaviors. The reward, the cue, has to be linked to what the dog did and not with you.

I see this initial elevated-bed training as killing three birds with one stone. First, as is true of all the behaviors I work on, the dog is offering it to me. Second, the dog has to move away from me in order to earn the reward, and I have to move toward him to provide the reward. That is a powerful moment of learning for the dog. Most often, behaviors are all about the dog being near the handler and receiving the reward. By rewarding a behavior in which the dog moves away from you, you are initiating an association within the dog's mind that he sometimes has to go and do something in order to be rewarded. Third, you're exposing the dog to a different kind of environment—in this case, the raised platform. As discussed earlier, exposing your dog early and often to as many different kinds of environments as possible—stairs, cars, and so on—will help him gain confidence and get over any fear of unknowns.

Generally, within only a few days I can get most dogs to respond to their name and the "place" signal or verbal command and run from as far as twenty feet to get onto the bed and then stay there. If I need to add "sit" or "down" once the dog is on the bed, it's an easy addition with the click and reward. Though the "place" command is more complicated than working on a single and simple command, it is like a key that unlocks a lot of doors for your dog. Dogs, like people, learn to learn. Once you've made that first breakthrough, the other aspects of learning and obedience will come more easily.

I'm often asked what to do when you start working with a dog and want to develop "sit" and the dog offers lying down. Do you still click and reward when the dog lies down instead of sits? The answer is yes if it is early in the dog's training. More important, that's a case of asking the wrong question. You don't go into a session with one single desired behavior in mind. You are looking for the dog to offer any of those from the list of basics—sit, stay, down, and so on—and so you would reward any of them.

Later on, when I want to be sure that the dog is really responding to my signal to sit (either a verbal command or a physical signal), I'll click and reward only when he responds correctly to that signal. Once you get to that point, you're changing the order of things to command/signal → desired behavior → click → reward.

At this more progressed stage, if I give a command/signal and the dog offers a different desired behavior, then I don't click and reward. I wait until the command/signal is executed properly. I've seen a lot of command/signal confusion with dogs; you have to make it clear to them that a particular sound and/or gesture means just that one single behavior.

You can also use a clicker to work on manners and boundaries. Let's say you are in the house and the doorbell rings and the dog doesn't go charging toward the door. Click and reward. You can set up all kinds of training scenarios to work on those common frustrations that people frequently have with their dogs.

ADDING ANOTHER DIMENSION

During basic training and introducing proper manners and respect for boundaries, you're primarily working alone with your dog in your neutral training area. In the real world, you are seldom going to experience such an isolated environment. Once you're satisfied with your dog's proper association and execution of desired behaviors in the training setting, it's time to move out into the real world. That means changing the location of the training. If you've been indoors for the most part, move outdoors. If you've kept the kids out of the house while working with the dog, let them be inside doing their thing.

Think of this as moving beyond the classroom and into the real world. You know from your own experiences that what you've learned in a classroom and applying that knowledge in a more practical setting can be very different. The same is true for your dog. Being able to recall, sit, stay, and so on in the classroom has its purpose, but you know that your dog is going to live most of his life outside that environment. You need to make sure that the classroom learning translates to as many different environments as possible. A simulation is a simulation, and in training you're going to be constantly simulating a real-world experience, but you should be progressing toward the more real as you advance.

You can create purposeful distractions as well as using the sights and sounds of being outdoors to enhance your dog's training. Having your kids toss a ball back and forth while you're working on the recall command, for example, is a great way to keep the dog focused on the task at hand. If you plan to include your dog in family outings to public places, then you definitely need to do some of the training sessions in places where your family is most likely to go.

You may end up feeling like you've taken one step forward and two steps back when you move into this phase of training. Here, as always, patience is key. It is far better to call off a session before you reach a level of frustration than it is to get to your breaking point. No good will come of you expressing your anger or dismay. There's also no point in pressing your dog into a training regimen that he can't enjoy or at least benefit from. Again, you've got to be able to read your dog and know when it simply isn't going to happen for that day or that particular session. I can't reinforce enough the idea that these training sessions should be enjoyable for you both, but especially for your dog. For the MWDs I train, running hundreds of yards and engaging in a battle with a man in a bite suit is enjoyable. Every dog will reveal what he likes to do at some point and you need to be able to read the signs when enough is enough (whether it is a good thing or no fun at all). Dogs have bad days just as you and I do.

ADAPT AND ADJUST AND REMAIN PATIENT

It will take your dog some time to simply adjust to a new environment. Some dogs are more adaptable than others. The more you expose your dog to different environments outside the classroom, and without actually engaging in a formal training session there, the more you reduce the amount of distraction. That means that taking your dog to a park or other open area a few times without getting involved in a training session will make it easier down the line when school's in session in a different location.

VARIABLE REWARD SCHEDULES

I'm not big into fancy terminology, but the concept of using variable reward schedules is important to firmly embed a concept in your dog's mind. What that means is that as you progress through the training of a behavior and it becomes very consistent, don't reward success every time. At this more advanced stage, you should get the dog to do the behavior a few times in succession but reward it with the big reward only on the last of two to three, or right in the middle. Reward him with praise for the previous completions, but give the larger reward—a treat, a toy, a chance to fetch—only at various intervals in that longer sequence.

You can also use this technique to reward only the best examples of that behavior. Some dogs "sloppy sit"—where one hip is thrown out to the side and their spine angle isn't straight. If you don't like

A proper "down" command being performed.

A proper "sit" command being performed.

that kind of sit, reward the dog only when he offers that good, fully erect, at-attention sit. The same is true with the incomplete or bounced-back "down." If you want your dog to lie down fully and remain there before coming back up, eventually, when the dog has a success ratio of nine out of ten, move on to only rewarding that best-case scenario.

LURING

In most instances, I don't recommend showing a dog a treat ahead of time as a way to get him to move into a desired location. However, you can use a treat as a bit of a shortcut. Hold the treat in front of the dog's nose, but don't let him take the treat from you. Begin moving toward the direction in which you want the dog to go.

The name for this type of training maneuver is *luring*, and it has all the potential drawbacks and negative associations that word has for us. With the emphasis on the reward rather than the behavior, you're not making as complete and as sound an association as you ideally would have. But with a dog who is reluctant, highly energized, or otherwise not properly focused, luring can be an effective tool.

CAPPING DRIVES

When you came up with ultimate goals while employing and thinking about the short term and the long term, that list should have included your dog performing the way that you wanted him to in any and all circumstances. I've talked about distractions and how to add them in. Another element to this do-it-all-the-time-regardless-of-the-circumstances training is something called *capping a drive*. This ultimately means that your dog should respond to your commands/signals regardless of how excited he is. The best way to envision this is when you go to the door to let your dog outside. His drive, his desire to be outside, is so strong that he may turn and spin and jump and bark and show other signs that his energy level is high. Even in that state of agitation, your dog should still respond appropriately to you.

Picture a bottle of soda. Normally, its contents are inert—they're just sitting inside that bottle. What happens when you shake it? They bubble and fizz. If you were to open it, it would fly out uncontrollably. With your dog, you want him, even under the most excited state, to still be under control. That's where the capping comes in.

You can begin this kind of training very early on. If you keep a puppy in a crate and you approach the crate, he may begin to jump up and down excitedly. If you immediately open the door and let him out—giving him what he wants, rewarding him—then he associates that excitable state with a desired behavior. How do you break that association? Simply by ignoring him and not letting him out until he calms down, stops jumping, and sits quietly. Then allow him out. That way, he will make the association that he gets the reward because of his calm state, not because he was in an excited state.

In some advanced training and dog sports, handlers will purposely arouse their dogs into that heightened state so that when they do perform their obedience work, they will go at it with great gusto.

That's not the goal for most of you training pets at home. If you reward your dog for that kind of high-energy behavior, he's going to continue to do it. I know of many people who like to see those displays of dog joy, and they're fine, but be sure to cap that display.

You can use the clicker to mark the calm state and then reward. The same basic principles apply here: Reward the desired behavior and ignore the undesired. This is just another variation on extinguishing a behavior.

ADDITIONAL CLICKER CONSIDERATIONS

It would get pretty annoying (not to mention noisy) if every clicker-training owner continued to use the device throughout the dog's life. The clicker is a training device. Once your dog demonstrates his competence with that behavior, then you can discontinue the use of the clicker with that behavior. You can always go back to using the clicker to reinforce learning. Eventually, you should get to the point where the clicker is no longer necessary. The only time you will use it is for maintenance work on previously learned behaviors, when working to extinguish an undesirable behavior that has cropped up, or when you want to teach a brand-new behavior.

As with humans as they age, mental stimulation remains important through all stages of a dog's life. I haven't addressed what we commonly refer to as "tricks," but they are another form of learned behavior that you can teach your dog to do. Not only is it possible to teach your dogs to perform tricks, but I believe that you should, regardless of the dog's age. I'm mostly concerned here with laying the foundation for teaching, so I won't go into great lengths about how to teach your dog to open the refrigerator to get you a beer, but the training principles I've laid out and will expand on further are all you need to figure out how to keep your dog mentally stimulated and yourself amused and entertained. Training is the time when that incredible bond between you and your dog really forms and solidifies. Why not keep that going throughout your relationship?

With what I've said about the sad state of dogs' fitness, you might think that clicker training and all those food rewards could be the culprit. Not all rewards have to be treats. Signs of affection, playing with a ball, and doing anything that the dog finds pleasurable and fun (as long as it isn't on your list of bad manners and violation of boundaries) can be used. If you do use food, keep in mind that for a fifty- to seventy-pound dog, that reward should be about half the size of a piece of bubble gum. For puppies, obviously, that food reward would be smaller, closer to the size of a pea.

Different-sized treats for different-sized dogs. Remember the size of the dog and the amount of reinforcement of a behavior you want to accomplish when choosing a treat size.

PUTTING IT ALL TOGETHER

I started this chapter by mentioning one of the most frequently asked questions I get. To demonstrate all of the points in this chapter, I'll take you through how we train dogs to run on a treadmill or to mount up in a helicopter. There are far more similarities than differences in how we approach the training for either scenario. Also, we are using the same basic principles that you would use to train your dog in everything from those basic manners to more involved "tricks." The fundamentals apply across the board.

The first of these similarities is that both devices are not something a dog would have any real familiarity with prior to my working with them. Because of that, it is important to make the dog's first experience around those objects a positive one. While a helicopter produces a hell of a lot more noise and motion than a treadmill, it's important that the dog's first exposure to either machine is while it is still and quiet.

I've done this training both with the use of a clicker and without, but in either case, I bring the dog around the machine. Generally, the dog will ignore it or perhaps give it a quick sniff and be done with it. That's fine. When he does approach it, handing out a reward of some kind helps build a positive association. With the MWDs that I've trained, that generally means using a ball and sometimes a few moments of playing fetch. A food treat would work as well. I don't want the dog to get too fired up about being near the object, but rather treat it as he would a tree, a piece of playground equipment at a park, or any other part of the environment.

That means that I have to keep my attitude neutral. I don't want to be too anxious and act like everything is on the line—that success or failure is a matter of life or death. Vocal cues or body language that express disappointment or frustration will only delay the real learning.

Next, I want to get the dog to not just be near the machine but to place on it. Again, this is still with the machine sitting there silent and unmoving. Reward as necessary—for coming close, to approaching being on it, to fully being on it. Here is where it sometimes becomes necessary to lure the dog. That said, if I've done my work early on the "place" command on that elevated bed, it is easier to get a dog to jump onto the deck of a treadmill or into a helicopter. If I've laid the groundwork of exposing a dog to a multitude of environments, this is easier.

You can guess what follows after the dog successfully jumps onto the treadmill on command. Amping up the distraction factor means turning on the machine and allowing the dog to adjust to the sounds and motions associated with the machine being in operation. This is a bit of a repeat of the first stage. I don't lump desensitizing the dog to the sensory stimuli with being on the machine. First do the sensory stuff and then add in the place location. I play with the dog or otherwise reward him while being near the now-functioning machine. Again, the point is to keep it positive.

With the helicopter, the next step is really the last one. The handler and the dog mount the bird. We do many repeats of takeoffs and landings. Because of the bond of trust that has been built up while reaching this point in their training, most MWDs take pretty easily to going aloft. The noise can be deafening and the sensations of

banking and turning and rising and falling somewhat disconcert-
ing, but because the dog is inside the calm bubble of his handler, he's
generally less excitable than he would be if he were loaded onto it in
a crate without his human teammate with him.

Getting a dog to stay on a treadmill's moving belt is more difficult than simply mounting a helicopter and then having it move.
Obviously, getting the dog to remain on the belt and facing the right
direction is aided by the use of a harness and leash. Having a dog
who is an eager runner also helps. But again, visualizing each of
the incremental steps you need to take and proceeding very slowly
and keeping your emotions in check will help make the transition
from housepet to gym rat. For some dogs, the sheer act of being able
to run will be reward enough. Moving the belt speed from its slow-
est crawl to a good pace will also help. For the first few times on a
moving treadmill, I recommend you keep to that slow crawl exclu-
sively. Offer ample rewards for when the dog moves his legs and
paws to keep pace with the belt.

So many variables play a part in how this will go for you and
your dog—not just with treadmill training but with all aspects of
training and enforcing manners and boundaries. I can't account for
every variable you will encounter, but with the right attitude and
demonstrable patience, coupled with proper reinforcement of the
desired behavior, you will achieve what you first envisioned. This is
the key to all training: positive associations and good timing with
reinforcement of the desired behaviors. It's really that simple. It
doesn't matter what you are training your dog to do; what matters
is that you put yourself in the dog's shoes and give him a reason to

do what you want, and a reason not to do what you don't want, by communicating those things in all of your actions.

THE WELL-TRAINED DOG

Just as it's impossible to be partially pregnant—a woman either is or she isn't—a dog isn't really trained unless he demonstrates the response to a command without fail. That's the goal and many people are able to attain it. You may have a slightly different set of expectations. Even if you do settle for less than 100 percent compliance, you should work toward getting your dog not just to "listen" to you, as many people put it, but to react to you nearly instantaneously.

What's the difference between listening and reacting? Well, if you've been paying attention, you know what I've been saying all along about placing yourself in your dog's perspective. You know that sounds and tone and volume are as important as the words themselves. You also know that dogs are simple-association animals. You want your dog to not just associate your commands with a reward, but to associate them with an action. When you repeat an action over and over, it becomes nearly involuntary. Your muscles just do it without any kind of real thought or premeditation. That's a reaction.

That's your goal.

In order to develop reactions, you have to experience multiple repetitions over a long period of time.

I know some people who played different ball sports for a long time. Surprise them by tossing a ball at their face and they'll likely be able to catch it. Someone who doesn't have that kind of long-term exposure and has to think about what to do will likely end up with a broken nose or a black eye.

Think of this another way. As SEAL team members, we drilled over and over again various weapons-firing scenarios. I got to a point where if I heard a click when I fired the trigger and neither felt nor heard the discharge of a round, I would, without any kind of thought, react by discarding that primary weapon, my long gun, and immediately reach for a secondary weapon. That was all muscle memory from hundreds and hundreds of correct repetitions.

When you say "sit" or wag a finger down, your well-trained dog will instantly, without hesitation, engage the muscles of his legs and back and put his butt on the ground. The same should be true for any and all of the various commands and tricks you want to teach him. As much as this book has talked about the mind of your dog and how his brain works and how to get his mind right to understand the authoritarian role you play in his life, ultimately our goals are about what your dog does and not what he thinks.

As with all things, practice makes perfect.

SIX

Care and Maintenance of Your Dog and Your Relationship

SEAL team members form a deep and lasting bond based on mutual respect and shared experience. In employing the methods of the Navy SEAL way, I hope that you and your dog will develop a similar kind of bond. Training is just one part of those shared experiences. I know that in addition to family members, I have a few other people in my life whom I can count on to help me when asked, and even when not asked. The brotherhood that we share has long outlasted the time we spent deployed or working together. Team members take care of one another, and that's an important part of forging the best possible relationship between you and your dog. This chapter and the one on fitness that follows present a detailed scheme for taking care of your dog. As I've pointed out before, the Navy SEAL mind-set is that details matter, that you have to look at both the short term and the long term, and that your situational awareness will help prevent problems from occurring.

In many ways, this information about health, nutrition, and fitness is as much about you training yourself as it is about you training your dog. When a MWD is deployed, before each operation the handler will go through a visual and tactile (hands-on) inspection of the dog to determine his state of fitness for the operation. Included in that will be more general observations. Examining each part of the dog's anatomy, noting his respiratory rate at rest, and other checks help ensure that the dog will be able to perform his job at peak efficiency.

For dogs as housepets, part of the bargain that you enter into after you've selected a dog is that you will take care of his physical needs. You have to use your situational awareness to pay attention to your dog and establish a kind of baseline standard to determine any variation from the dog's normal appearance, attitude, and physical capabilities—everything from how he walks and runs to his level of energy and activity.

With your dog, you don't have to do the kind of checks a MWD's handler does every day in such detail, but you do need to be as observant as the MWD's handler. The baseline standard that you will determine is no different from what a MWD's handler would track. While your dog's level of physical fitness is likely to be well below that of a SEAL team dog, and his level of activity and energy will also be lower, the kinds of anatomical checks you should perform periodically are the same. From tip to tail, your dog's body is sending you signals about his operational status. Obviously, a dog can't tell you verbally how he's feeling—with some exceptions like whimpering when in severe pain—so it's up to you to really be your dog's best friend and get to read the signs that indicate when he is feeling off. You should be doing this when your dog is a puppy or when you first acquire him and throughout the rest of his life.

Not only is paying proper attention to the care and feeding of your dog humane, it pays dividends for you in the long run. A healthy and physically fit dog will be easier to work with in training and will behave better generally. Think about how difficult it is for you to perform at your best when you are ill, sore, sleep deprived, hungry, or otherwise not at 100 percent physically. Just as very young children can't verbalize what might be hurting or bothering them and will let you know in other ways, so do dogs. It's up to you to develop the proper situational awareness to know the normal baseline behavior and appearance of your dog and pay close enough attention to notice and intervene when any variation from that baseline occurs. There are many reasons why your dog might seem distracted in training and underperform. Your awareness of your dog's physical condition will help determine the potential cause of that. Feeding your dog in a nutritionally sound manner and giving him the proper amount of exercise will make it easier for him to behave well in the classroom and to learn better during training.

NOSE

While it's true that a dog's nose is usually damp and cool, that is not a definite indicator that he is in good health. Neither is a dry, warm nose. You should pay attention to the state of the dog's nose and detect any wide variations—dry and cracked or unusually runny.

There's also no absolute correlation between the state of a dog's nose and his temperature. If you want to know if your dog has a fever, take his rectal temperature. A dog's temperature should be between 101 and 102.5 degrees Fahrenheit. That is about two to four degrees higher than our own, so when you are in close contact with your dog and you note that he feels warmer than you, that's normal.

EYES

A dog's eyes should be shiny and bright. Some occasional light discharge and watery tears are normal, but any discoloration of those fluids indicates an issue. Any kind of swelling, inflammation, or discharge from the pink lining around the eyelids is also abnormal. A yellow-tinged sclera (the white part of the eye) is also a warning sign of some underlying issue.

For the pupils of your dog's eyes, a general principle applies. While the size of a dog's pupils may be different from one dog to the next, in an individual dog, symmetry rules. (That is true for much of a dog's anatomy.) If one of your dog's pupils is larger than the other, that's a strong indication that something is not right, anything from head trauma to infections to exposure to chemicals. You can try to flush your dog's eyes using eye flush solution or water, but if the problem persists beyond a day or two, it is best to consult with a veterinarian. You can clean any discharge from around your dog's eyes with a clean and damp cotton ball or baby wipe, being careful not to come into contact with the eyeball itself and working from the outside to the center.

The same is true if you shine a light in your dog's eyes individually and note that they respond differently in terms of dilating or constricting—consult with a veterinarian.

TEETH

Any dentist will likely tell you that good health begins inside the mouth. That is where we take in nutrition, and a healthy mouth contributes to digestive health, which contributes to the health of the rest of our organs and tissues. That is also true for dogs. Any abscesses/infections in the mouth can easily spread, particularly to the heart, so it's important to check the status of your dog's mouth. Depending on the dog, that coloration will range from pink to black to spotted with colors similar to his skin—not his coat. No matter the color of the gums, the flesh should be firm. Any kind of regular bleeding or discharge from the teeth and gums is an obvious sign of trouble. If your dog's gums are white, or if they are brighter pink/red, you should contact your veterinarian. Both of those color variations are signs of other possible issues such as low blood pressure, blood-borne parasites, internal bleeding in the case of white/pale gums, or fever or infection in the case of red gums.

Dogs who eat dry food are exposed to greater buildup on the teeth. Severe tartar and plaque buildup can lead to gum disease down the line. Brushing your dog's teeth several times a week will help prevent this problem from worsening, will help control breath odor, and serves as a bonding/trust exercise.

Because a dog's mouth serves many different functions—feeding, drinking, protection, pleasure (chewing/biting)—it is important to check your dog's mouth and tongue regularly. Surprisingly, many dog owners neglect to do this as a part of good general maintenance. With the MWDs and personal protection dogs I train, the mouth is a source of protection and apprehension, so we pay a great deal of attention to it; you and your dog would also benefit from that level of detailed examination.

Things to Look For:

- Bad breath
- Loose teeth
- Excessive drooling or drooling that varies from the normal amount
- Inflammation of the gums
- Tumors
- Cysts under the tongue

Chew toys, bones, and sticks will all help keep your dog's mouth healthy, and as with humans, sugars and starches that remain on the teeth cause decay. Your veterinarian can also perform teeth cleanings, and I highly recommend them.

THE EAR

There are nearly as many words used to describe the various shapes of ears that dogs possess as there are breeds. Okay, maybe that's a bit of an exaggeration, but for our purposes it's best to keep things simple. Some dogs normally have a flap over the middle and inner parts of the ear and others don't. Generally, dogs whose ears are covered require a bit more attention because moisture, dirt, and wax can build up in the inner folds more easily.

Healthy wax is pale gray to light brown; excessive or discolored wax can be a sign of an infection. So can a foul odor coming from the ears. The skin covering the floppy part of the ear should be pale—pink and red are negative indicators. The inner part of the flap should, however, be pink or red. Excessive head shaking or scratching of the ears will alert you to a potential problem.

Consult with your veterinarian about what kind of ear-cleaning products to use and how frequently to use them. Overuse of cleaning solutions can damage your dog's hearing.

THE COAT

Caring for your dog's coat is more than a cosmetic issue; a healthy coat makes a dog more comfortable and less prone to skin complaints and problems with parasites. Some dogs have a single coat, while others have a double coat—an undercoat (generally lighter colored) with short, soft, dense hair, and a longer and coarser (in comparison to the undercoat) outer coat. Dogs who don't shed their coat (breeds that originated in colder climates) require a bit more maintenance so that undercoat doesn't get too thick and matted.

No matter what type of coat your dog has—single or double; coarse or smooth; wiry, curly, straight, short, or long—it should be glossy and pliable. It should also be free of dandruff, bare patches, and excess oil.

I'm not going to spend time on how to care for a dog's coat, but I do want to point out that running your hand over your dog's coat to check it also provides you with an opportunity to detect any kinds of lumps or other abnormalities that lie underneath that coat. Also, while running your hand along your dog's body, you can press against joints—hips, elbows, ankles—to see if that probing produces a pain/discomfort response in your dog. The more active your dog is, the more frequently you should do this. Think of this as purposeful petting—using your situational awareness to head off any potential problems.

PAWS

Ideally, you and your dog will be getting lots of exercise, so that means that paws on the ground will be a regular part of your dog's day. Keep in mind that the pads of a dog's paws perform an important function—they act as a cushion that helps protect joints from being overloaded as well as cushioning softer tissues of the paw while on rough surfaces. They also provide your dog with protection from extremes of hot and cold. Cracked and dry pads can and should be moisturized. Consult with your veterinarian about the best products to use for that.

The other part of your dog's paw that requires attention and maintenance are his nails. Unless your dog walks outside on pavement with enough regularity to grind them down so that they reach ideal length on their own—fractionally above the ground—they will require trimming. This is something you can do on your own, at your vet's office, or at a groomer's.

You should also check regularly for objects that can become lodged or stuck in between the dog's paw pads. In addition, trimming the hair between the pads is another part of maintenance and prevention. Cutting it even with the pads themselves will prevent matting of the fur, make it less likely that an object will get attached, and in climates where snow is prevalent, it will lessen the chances of frozen buildup. Melting agents used on roads and sidewalks are harsh chemicals and it's a good idea to rinse your dog's paws after a winter walk.

Again, as part of your situational awareness, focus on harmful debris—broken glass, thorns, thistles, burrs, and so on—and lead your dog around those potentially harmful areas. Prevention is a better option than treatment of injuries.

WASTE PRODUCTS

Another important indicator of your dog's overall health is the waste that he eliminates. Urine should be a clear yellow—darker colors are an indication that the dog is dehydrated, and reddish yellow may indicate that blood is in the urine. The color of the urine is a direct reflection of kidney function.

Checking the state of your dog's feces is equally essential. Solid fecal matter, predominately brown or yellowish brown in color, is ideal. Noting the frequency and condition of your dog's eliminations will help you determine if anything is at variance from the norm. Stress and changes in environment can affect stool production, so it is important to look for longer-term trends rather than a single incident of either loose or too-firm/dry stool.

Your dog also has a pair of anal glands—one on each side of his rectum. Those glands produce a distinctive odor that dogs use to identify another dog's gender, age, health status, and other pieces of information. Functionally, the anal glands and sac should secrete some of the fluid produced when your dog has a bowel movement. In some dogs, because of either a structural malformation or a poor diet, those fluids don't get expressed, or released, and the pressure becomes an irritant. A dog scooting his butt or licking or chewing excessively at his hind end are both indicators that the anal glands may be causing a problem. You can either take your dog to the vet or learn how to express those glands yourself.

A DOG'S GAIT

How your dog moves will help you better understand the state of his muscles and his skeletal system. Just as humans have unique ways of walking and running, so do dogs. In its purest form, your dog's gait, like his body development, should be symmetrical. That means that the left and right sides should essentially be mirror images of each other whether the dog is at rest or moving. But just as there's no perfect symmetry in humans, the same is true for dogs. Some imbalance will result in slight distortions of that mirror image. Any more noticeable differences between the left and right sides can produce what experts call "lameness." That doesn't mean that the animal is so impaired that movement is difficult or impossible, just that he varies from the normal state.

When you observe your dog, you will again notice his tendencies. Some dogs move in a more or less straight line with the tip of their nose and their tail moving on the same plane. Some dogs have a more side-to-side gait with the head at, let's say, the twelve o'clock position and the rear end to either side of six o'clock. If that is the dog's normal gait, there's no reason to be concerned. If the dog is normally a twelve-to-six dog and starts to move outside that alignment, that may be a sign that the dog is favoring one of his limbs.

There are two types of lameness: anatomical and pathological. Anatomical lameness is not a result of pain. It is a product of genetics or it can be acquired. Pathological lameness can be a symptom of neurological or anatomical musculoskeletal issues. Since dogs have four legs, they have the ability to compensate for difficulties with one of their limbs, which can often mask an underlying issue. Sometimes those compensations can lead to strains in other parts of the body. You've likely heard stories of athletes who've injured one part of their body and made some alteration in how they moved to compensate for the original injury, and in the process ended up hurting something else.

Any of the joints can be vulnerable to malformations and/or injury, but within certain breeds, the hips are particularly prone to problems. In selecting a dog, particularly one from a breeder, be sure to ask for x-rays and certifications of the soundness of a dog's hips, meaning he is less prone to develop the inherited disorder known as hip dysplasia. That malformation of the hips results in the head of the femur (the leg bone that fits into the hip socket) grinding against another bone. Not every instance of a dog experiencing some stiffness after lying prone, demonstrating a reluctance or inability to jump up, or having a decrease in physical activity associated with hip issues is certain to be caused by dysplasia.

Common sense should rule the day, and if your dog demonstrates any sign of lameness, particularly after hard periods of exercise, it is likely a result of overuse. Rest and modified activity are the best course of action. If the problem persists, then it may be time for medical intervention.

Hip dysplasia is an inherited condition, so there's no cure. Keeping your dog's weight down; exercising sensibly to help strengthen the muscles around the joint; massage, heat, and ice; anti-inflammatory medications; and all the other treatments that you would employ to help yourself overcome a joint issue are appropriate for your dog as well. Swimming is a great non-weight-bearing exercise with the benefits of full range of motion.

START EARLY, DO IT REGULARLY, WORK PATIENTLY, AND KEEP YOUR EMOTIONS IN CHECK

I'm sure that some of you either flinched at the thought of checking and expressing your dog's anal glands or thought there is no way in hell your dog would tolerate that kind of treatment.

The four points I made in the heading of this section will ensure that in most cases your dog will allow you to perform any of the kinds of checks and maintenance activities I've just listed, just as he allows his vet to do them. Though it was the last one listed, I believe that the most important of these is to keep your emotions in check. If you become impatient and frustrated with your dog's initial unwillingness to cooperate, if you project any kind of fear, anxiety, or disgust, your dog will pick up on your heightened and negative emotional state, and that will make these relatively simple tasks anguishing, if not impossible, for you and your dog. Think about your own experience with the medical professionals you've had work on your body. You need to project the same kind of confident and in-control demeanor as the best doctors do when they treat you. Being too comforting and overexaggerating your care and compassion can also send a dog a signal that something out of the ordinary is going on. A routine, matter-of-fact, we're-going-to-be-doing-this-all-the-time, cavalier approach is best.

If you begin doing the kinds of inspections that I listed previously early in the dog's life or in your relationship with an older dog, and you combine them with that professional and caring demeanor, your dog will respond in kind. It also helps to not simply dive in. As is true with the training methodology I recommend, you have to be patient and work up to some of the complicated tasks.

Apply that same gradual baby-step process to any prevention and treatment and offer rewards for compliance, and in turn you will build trust, let your dog know that you are the go-to person to help ease his pain, and save yourself some money on vet bills. You know that you've built a solid foundation of trust with your dog when he communicates that he is having an issue. People have reported to me that their dog will come to them, sit, and offer his paw, letting them know that there is something imbedded or stuck in his paw.

Your dog is looking for that kind of care from you, and with patience and a firm resolve to remain calm and patient and in control, you'll be able to provide most of his care on your own. When in doubt, consult your veterinarian.

DIET AND NUTRITION

If there's an area in which even the most loving and conscientious dog owners are guilty of neglecting their dog's best interests, this is it. We are a nation at risk of killing ourselves off due to poor diet, and we're at risk of doing the same to our dogs. The National Institutes of Health (NIH) reported in 2013 that the United States finished last among seventeen nations assessed for life expectancy among men and second to last among women. Another recent report cited that, metabolically, the present generation of American adults is fifteen years older than previous generations. I could go on and cite even more statistics about the declining health of the American population, but I'll leave it at this: If we are doing these things to ourselves, and many of them are attributable to poor diet and exercise habits, then imagine what we are doing to our dogs. Presumably, you care more about your own personal health than you do your dog's, and many people consider a dog a part of the family, so what does that mean for dogs?

A lean, healthy dog; notice the slight tuck from the rib cage up into the hips.

This dog is at the beginning stages of being overweight. If your dog is this heavy or heavier, you need to feed less and exercise more.

BODY MASS INDEX AND CANINES

Body mass index (BMI) uses a human's height and weight as part of a calculation that produces a number that correlates to the amount of fat on a person's body. Because weight issues have become so prevalent in the canine world, as well as among felines, several research organizations have begun developing similar kinds of BMI calculators for pets. As I write this, none is reliably available.

In addition, veterinarians may now use something called the *body condition scoring* (BCS) metric. The Ohio State University College of Veterinary Medicine has an online illustrated chart (http://vet.osu.edu/vmc/body-condition/scoring-chart) that gives you some idea of how you can rank your dog. This is based on your observation of your dog's appearance. Veterinarians commonly use BCS scales, one that rates dogs from one to five and another that uses a nine-point scale.

It might seem that just looking at a dog's appearance is too subjective, but studies have shown a link between the BCS scores and body fat percentage. The ideal BCS on the five-point scale is three. For the nine-point scale the ideal is four or five. According to veterinary science researchers at a number of institutions, those numbers correspond to a body fat percentage somewhere between 15 and 25 percent, and a body fat measurement within that range is also considered ideal.

While researchers are looking into inexpensive ways to measure a dog's body fat percentage, you should consult your vet or possibly a local university's school of veterinary medicine to see about these new approaches. BCS at least gives you some sense of your dog's body fat percentage. Any Internet search for canine body fat measurement will produce some interesting results.

Maintaining an ideal BCS score is essential at all times, but particularly as your dog ages. Too high a percentage of body fat and/or excess weight puts greater stress on a dog's organs and joints.

When it comes to your dog's overall health, despite any genetic predispositions and/or present conditions, you have control over the most important aspects of his health and longevity—an optimal diet and sufficient exercise. I've known few dogs who are self-regulating when it comes to food intake. Given their history on the planet and their genetic inheritance, it makes sense that dogs are opportunistic feeders—they will eat as much as they can when they can. Consequently, it's up to you to monitor their intake. That may seem an obvious point, but go to any dog park or other place where dogs are gathered in numbers, and you will likely see an astounding percentage of overweight dogs. A recent survey indicated that 53 percent of all dogs in this country are overweight.

Being overweight and obese can lead to joint issues and heart, liver, skin, and respiratory disease, as well as act as a contributing factor in heatstroke. Any way you look at it, a dog who is lean is healthier than one who is overweight.

Because of the large variation in sizes of dogs, it would be excessive for me to provide you with a table that shows the ideal weight, body fat percentage, body mass index (BMI), or other metrics that we use as humans to determine whether we are overweight or obese. For dogs, we mostly use a kind of rule-of-thumb appearance check to determine this. Most dogs who are fit will show a little of both their ribs and hip bones, just as is true of fit human beings. There should be a tuck from the rib cage to the hips as well. This looks like a curve inward, with the rib cage wider than the waist: a classic hourglass shape.

One of the hesitations that I have about presenting this method of checking your dog's weight is that it relies almost entirely on your visual sense and determination. Whenever I have visitors who see my dogs, they frequently say something like, "Wow! That dog is so skinny!" In fact, I monitor my dogs' weight very carefully, and they are fit and healthy and not in any way underfed or undernourished. It's just that we've become so accustomed to seeing overweight dogs (and people) that the observational norm that many people operate from is out of whack with the reality of what a healthy, well-fed, and fit person or dog should look like.

With rare exceptions, the reason a dog is overweight is simple: His owner feeds him too much. We often kill dogs with our kindness, and every time I hear someone say, "I feel so bad for my dog. He seems hungry all the time," I feel like saying (and sometimes do say), "You should be feeling sorry for the dog's heart, liver, kidneys, and joints that you're helping to destroy."

Part of your role as the authority figure in your relationship is to take command and control of your impulses. Letting your heart get too much in the way of your head and what's best for your dog will end up causing that heart more pain in the long run. Also, remember this—going hungry can be a little uncomfortable; being overweight or obese is downright dangerous.

DOG FOOD AND NUTRITION

Despite an entire industry built around weight loss, the basic underlying principle is simple. If a dog (or human) is overweight, that's the result of consuming too many calories for the body to handle efficiently. That means that one or two things must happen: Take in fewer calories and/or burn off more calories. The pet food industry has made a lot of advances in its less than one-hundred-year existence. I believe that most of those have to do with convenience. The labels provided on dog food give you a good idea of what is inside and how much you should generally give your dog based on his weight. There are lots of variables surrounding your dog's activity level, metabolic rate, and so on, so treat those guidelines for what they are—guidelines, or a mere starting point. Always assume that you're going to think your dog is thinner than he really is. It's far better to err on the side of feeding too little than it is to feed too much.

What Your Dog Should Eat

Dogs are carnivores. While there is some debate about the fact that they are omnivores, their eating of vegetable matter is an adaptation borne of desperation and not design. A quick look at their teeth will tell you that. Nearly every one of their teeth is a spike or a serrated triangle. They don't have square molars or rounded flat teeth. They are designed to eat whole, dead, raw animals—including bones.

Many dog owners have good success with feeding their dogs dry food. I can't quibble with that too much, but I'm not an advocate of dry food for dogs. I will say this about dry dog food. It contains everything your dog needs. It is incredibly convenient and provides you as your dog's caretaker with a kind of thought-free assurance that your dog is getting what he needs to survive and maintain relative good health.

That said, feeding your dog dry food is like surviving on beef jerky and canned goods. You'd stay alive, but that doesn't mean that the food is particularly good for you. Just as we are learning more and more how bad processed foods are for humans, it stands to reason that the highly processed nature of dry dog food is not the best for our dog's health or longevity either. It's good that additives are introduced to enrich nutritional value, but that fact should tell you something about the overall effectiveness of the food in the first place. It is the equivalent of us taking a multivitamin and other supplements. We do that because the foods we eat aren't sufficient to provide what we need.

IT'S NOT HOW MUCH BUT WHAT KIND

Without getting bogged down in too many details, there are good proteins and bad proteins. Good proteins are easy to break down into the twenty-two amino acids your dog needs to be healthy. A dog's body can produce twelve of those twenty-two amino acids, which means he has to get the rest from the food he eats. Some proteins in food are indigestible—your dog's body can't break them down into anything usable. (That's why soy and corn are on the no-no list presented a bit later.) For example, the protein in beaks, feet, hides, tails, and snouts contains 100 percent protein but is also 100 percent indigestible. These parts can go on the label as a contribution to the protein percentage in the food, but they don't go into your dog's body as usable amino acids. Low-quality proteins just tax the digestive system and don't contribute much.

Nutritionists talk about a food's *biologic value*—how much of it a body can break down into useful components. Eggs have the highest biologic value at 100 percent. Fish has a biologic value of 92 percent. Most animals don't eat feathers, mostly because they have an unappealing texture, but they also have no biologic value.

The key concept here is to have species-appropriate food available for your dog. Such food will have the highest biologic content and produce the least amount of

metabolic stress—that means it should be whole, raw, un-
processed, and in its natural form.

I feed my dogs raw food and fully believe in its benefits. I understand that it can potentially be more expensive and is definitely less
convenient to feed a dog a raw diet. It requires more legwork on your
part to research and acquire what you need to feed raw effectively.
Entire books are devoted to the subject, and I will return briefly to
feeding dogs raw in a bit. For now, I'll make this statement and move
on: The best diet for a dog is one that mimics as closely as possible
what dogs ate while in the wild. While we've domesticated dogs and
we've had a great deal of impact on their genetic history, their organs
and structures of digestion—from their teeth to their asses—haven't
evolved.

What to Look for in Dry Food

When examining dry dog food's ingredients, here's a list of red-
flag ingredients. If you see the following, put the food back on the
shelf:

- Corn
- Soy
- Wheat
- Gluten (in any form)
- Beet pulp

- BHA
- BHT

BHA and BHT are chemicals added to food to prevent spoilage and have no nutritional value. Beet pulp is a filler that is supposed to provide additional fiber—which your dog doesn't really need.

The first ingredients listed should be a good source of meat protein—beef, chicken, lamb, or turkey. (I tend to stay away from products that use pork.) But be aware of the amount of protein that exists in the food as well. Too high a percentage of protein is not good—anything over 30 percent is excessive and will tax your dog's liver and kidneys.

Be wary of all grains and filler carbohydrates. Why no grains at all? Predomesticated or early-period domesticated dogs ate animals. The only grain that they might have eaten was in the stomach contents of what they had killed. A dog's digestive system can handle grains, but that returns us to the basic point: Do we want to feed them what they can handle or what's best for them? I have recently been pleased to see many more grain-free foods available in stores. Look for them!

Even when dry dog food isn't loaded with additives, it is still highly processed to make it dry. This dehydration of dog food can, in some cases, contribute to bloat. Dogs who eat dry food require more water. What can you do to counteract the effect of the drying process? Obviously, keeping an ample supply of water on hand for your dog is key.

Also watch out for grain-free dry foods that contain too high a percentage of protein. Again, look at that label. If the nutrient

percentages listed show a protein value of higher than 32 to 40 percent, don't use that food. In my experience, 26 percent protein is
ideal. Why? Because a greater percentage than that will tax your
dog's kidneys and liver, the organs that process protein and other
essential nutrients and make them available to the body. Add in the
fact that dry dog food has water content somewhere in the 12 to 70
percent range (as opposed to raw food, which is 80 percent water),
and that worsens the problems your dog's kidneys and liver will
have in processing protein. Not to be too cynical, but do you really
think that a high-protein dog food will also contain a high percentage of good (digestible and usable) proteins? No. Therefore the liver
and kidneys will be working overtime extracting and eliminating
good and bad proteins. That's not the case with a raw meat-based
diet.

Just as humans learned about the high-protein/low-carbohydrate
Atkins-like or paleo diet, veterinarians and dog food companies have
also made a push in that direction. A high-protein dry food works

Raw food versus dry food: There is no comparison.

for dogs if it contains 70 to 80 percent water. Anything less than that and the advantages are far outweighed by the disadvantages.

Fat

For a long time fat was the culprit. We forget that fat is essential to good health. Good fat in the right amount is absolutely necessary, particularly if your dog is going to be very active. When you look at the extremes of dog endurance activity, such as the Iditarod sled dog competition, some mushers feed their dogs very high amounts of animal tallow. Why? Because it is the best fuel source to combat the cold temperatures, especially for days on end, when the dogs are moving in excess of fourteen hours a day.

I provide my active working dogs with a diet that consists of 24 percent fat. These are dogs that are highly active. If I were making a dog food, I would have it contain 20 percent protein and 24 percent fat. I've been able to find commercially available foods that reverse that—24 percent protein and 20 percent fat. Many non-high-performance dry foods have fat percentages below 10 percent. While I don't recommend a 24 percent fat ratio for most housepets, if you are planning on doing strenuous activity with your dog, increase the fat you provide for him.

In summary, if you are going to feed dry dog food, look for:

- Protein in the 20 to 26 percent range
- The highest moisture content you can find (something close to the 80 percent that raw food contains)
- None of the ingredients on the no-no list

- The fewest, if any, grains
- If you go grain free, be sure to look at both the protein percentage and the moisture content.
- The more active your dog, the higher the fat ratio he needs.

A Brief Look at Feeding Raw

Raw means raw. Feeding your dog human food that has been cooked is not the same thing and does not provide the same benefits as feeding raw. When you cook meat, you take some of the moisture out of it. Besides, the point of feeding raw is to mimic the natural state of a dog's feeding existence. You want to get as close as you can to feeding him whole, raw animals. That means bones, flesh, sinew, and organs. That means things like eyes, lungs, and trachea. Those things aren't easy to find, and they shouldn't be the staple of the diet, anyway. Meat, bone, and flesh are the big three that I feed my dogs, with those other parts of a carcass once or twice a week.

My dogs' digestive systems have not responded well to pork, but domesticated meat animals, as well as game animals—rabbit, elk, deer, buffalo, caribou, and moose—have served my dogs well. I also believe in feeding dogs semifrozen portions of meat and bone. That way I have fewer worries about bone shards. Defrosted meat with bones doesn't break up as easily, so dogs will swallow larger portions and the chance of something getting lodged in their throats increases. If you've ever doubted the power of a dog's jaws, watch him work away at a frozen piece of flesh and bone.

To mimic the stomach contents of a downed animal a dog might ingest, I rely on vegetables—peas, spinach, broccoli, kale. I prefer to purée these vegetables rather than serve them whole. Dogs would have never eaten those foods in their whole state, so I don't feed them to my dogs that way, but it is beneficial for them to have them in a state similar to the partially digested stomach contents of an animal they would have fed on.

The dogs eat predominantly the protein sources and a much smaller percentage of the puréed vegetables. Good, full-service stand-alone butcher shops are becoming more rare, but they are the best source for your dog's raw food needs. I also supplement my feedings with a sprinkling of bone dust—think of this like the sawdust that is created when a blade goes through a piece of wood . . . but with bone instead of wood! This is a good source of calcium and other nutrients and can be used to help firm up a dog's stool.

Another good food that can help with a dog's digestive issues is canned pumpkin. If a dog is having trouble with vomiting or diarrhea, a few ounces of canned pumpkin can offer relief. Though I have not done this myself, I have heard that some veterinarians recommend "the pumpkin diet" to help overweight dogs. Again, consult with your veterinarian before moving forward with any one weight-loss plan for your dog.

Tallow and other forms of fat trimmings are available from butchers, but you have to make arrangements in advance with them because they generally discard it as scrap. Any skins that you might trim off chicken or turkey or fish are also a good source of fat. I also ask butchers to reserve whole cow livers for me. I cut them into bite-sized chunks, freeze them, and use them as treats. If I'm using beef liver for food, I provide it in quantity only a couple of times a week.

As training rewards, I use much smaller chunks. You can do the same with other animal parts that are typically discarded, such as organ meats and other parts that humans don't eat.

Why Raw?

- It mimics what your dog's ancestors ate naturally.
- It has the proper amount of moisture.
- You can control the percentages of nutrients to get the exact mix of fat, protein, and so on in your dog's diet.
- If you see a deficiency in your dog's appearance or performance, you can adjust the percentage of nutrients to compensate. For example:
  - Dull full coat—more fat
  - Joint pain—more bone/calcium
  - Low energy—more fat
- Raw food has no additives, preservatives, or chemicals.

A few words here in terms of cost. This goes back to thinking near-term and long-term. Yes, the per-pound price of raw meat versus a bag of dry dog food is going to be higher. But you will have to feed your dog less of that raw food in order to get the proper nutrients. Yes, if you have to buy a freezer, a meat grinder, and specialty knives or anything else that contributes to food overhead costs, your initial costs will climb. But if you look long-term, those expenses will be covered in terms of lower vet bills, more so if you have more than one dog at a time or over your life span. You also can't put a price on the quality of your dog's life and how much better he feels and performs when fed raw.

Obviously, this is a quick and dirty look at raw food. If you are interested in implementing this kind of diet with your dog, plenty of resources are available online or at your bookstore.

SEVEN

Fitness and Fun and Their Multiple Rewards

Because most dogs once did work for human beings, the concept of having to provide structured exercise time is a recent development in the history of human/canine relationships. The same kind of shift in the type of work that humans do has also necessitated that we go to gyms, lift weights, run, or do other cardiovascular workouts. The concept of "working out" would be foreign to a lot of our human ancestors whose physical labors left them with neither the time nor the energy to do additional kinds of physical activity. They wanted to do one of two things when not engaged in their work—have fun or rest.

THE HALO EFFECT

Any Internet search for the benefits of owning a dog will produce many results: lowered blood pressure, reduced

stress, increased activity level, higher community/sociabi-
lity, lessened mortality rates after a heart attack, kids who
read aloud to their dog showing a 12 percent improvement
in reading skills compared to those who do not, and the list
goes on and on. We have a serious health crisis in this country. Relative activity is a part of modern life, I suppose, and
merely having a dog present in your household has benefits.

If you extend that beyond your dog's presence to the
benefits you derive from having a dog to be active with,
then dogs are worth their weight and more in terms of
health benefits for humans. Among the many interesting
facts and findings:

- The *Journal of Physical Activity & Health* published a
  report that demonstrated that dog owners are more
  likely to reach their fitness goals than those without
  canine companions.
- Michigan State University researchers found that dog
  owners are 34 percent more likely to fit in 150 minutes
  of walking per week than non–dog owners.
- The same study revealed that dog ownership increased
  leisure-time physical activity by 69 percent.
- A University of Missouri study showed that people walk
  28 percent faster when walking with a dog as
  compared to 4 percent faster with another human.
- Walking your dog can reduce your risk of diabetes by
  one third.

- Teens from dog-owning families get an extra fifteen minutes of exercise per week compared to teens from dogless households.
- A UCLA study of the elderly showed that dog owners required 20 percent less medical care than non–dog owners.

Clearly, having a dog and being active with him will help you and your family improve your quality of life.

In some ways, that's true for dogs, as well. While we contemporary humans think of exercise as a form of work, for most dogs, exercise can and should be a form of play. For a lot of people, the exercise programs they engage in are purposeful in the sense that they help keep them physically and mentally fit but aren't purposeful in the sense that they don't engage in exercise as a way to be better at a particular activity, sport, or work function. In this brief chapter on exercise, I'll refer to *purposeful exercise*, a term that covers both of those things—what we can call exercise for exercise's sake and the health benefits we receive as a reward for those efforts, and the exercise we may do to enhance our lives by engaging in activities that we may take seriously but also bring us enjoyment or fun.

The SEAL teams are well known and highly regarded for a number of things. The fitness routines we perform are legendarily difficult for good reason. They were grueling, but they weren't difficult just for the sake of being difficult. Nearly everything we did in our training would prove useful to us when deployed and actively engaged in an operation. Many times, endurance was as much a question of pushing our mental stamina to new limits as it was doing so physically, if not more so. While I hesitate to say that dogs are as goal oriented as humans, I've seen how competitive they can be and how their desire to capture someone who is fleeing, to be ahead of another dog while walking, and so on brings them a great deal of satisfaction.

While the previous chapter focused on a dog's physical health, in talking about exercise and fitness, the mental aspect of your dog's life is important to consider as well. In some ways, that also is true for you and your mental state. If you've owned a dog before, or been around people who have a dog, you've heard or said some variation of this statement, "A tired dog is a good dog." Many people bring their dogs to a dog run or other public place where dogs are free to move about and mingle because they want to tire out their dog so that he will be calmer at home. There's absolutely nothing wrong with that; exercise is good, and dogs with a high energy level can use that energy to do something either productive or unproductive. Those unproductive activities—chewing things they shouldn't, excessive pacing/running/jumping, and a host of other behavioral issues—can also cause you some mental anguish.

Exercise for your dog and for you is part of that mutually beneficial relationship I talked about from the very beginning. I know few dogs who, depending on environmental factors, don't want to go for at least moderate walks regularly. As I said in the chapter on selecting the right kind of dog for you, matching your interests and activity level with a dog's is important. I wouldn't force a dog to participate in moderate to vigorous exercise if he is unwilling, uninterested, or incapable. On the other hand, I think that not exercising a dog who is willing, interested, and capable is also being unfair to him.

It's also important to match the dog's baseline fitness and health to the level of activity that you're going to engage in. Age is also a factor. As dogs grow older, like us, their ability to recover from muscle and joint strain becomes increasingly compromised, just as those joints and muscles become more susceptible to strain and more serious injury. Some dogs will tell you enough is enough, but many won't until it is too late. Because dogs are so focused on the moment, they don't have the same sense that we do (some of the time) to understand that if they are highly active and pushing themselves hard, there could be a price to pay the next day and beyond. You have to be the best judge of that for them. You have to strike a balance between being an advocate for your dog and getting him to do what you know is best for him (for example, in the case of an overweight dog who is a reluctant exerciser) and allowing him to have input. In general, short walks for any dog will be beneficial to his physical and mental state.

DOG WALKING BASICS

As is true with every part of dog training, how you carry yourself will make all the difference in the world in the results you get. Your posture/carriage, the authoritative tone you take with your body language, and the no-nonsense approach you take with your dog will signal that this is a time for him to be attentive. If you make too

Ideally, when you walk your dog, he should be aligned with his shoulder to your knee and slack in the leash.

This is an all-too-common sight that demonstrates exactly how not to walk your dog.

big a deal about it being time for a walk, rile the dog up in some way with actions and vocalizations that indicate that this is time for out-of-control fun, then you're likely to get a hard-charging, leash-pulling, I'm-choking-sounding dog. I have no doubt you've got a picture in your mind of what this walk shouldn't look like. Let's focus on what it should look like.

Ideally, when walking with your dog, you want him to maintain the same pace as you do. I'm not as much of a stickler for "the dog must be on your left and immediately at your side" as you might think—as it applies to housepets. Once respect is established, I believe it is fine for your dog to move a little ahead of you or to be immediately alongside you. You have to decide what level of attentiveness you want to command in this arena. I don't, however, think it's acceptable for a dog to be straining fully at the leash and for you to be trying to hold him back. That's no fun for you, but it may be fun for your dog and you'd be rewarding that dog's desire to pull by letting that go on. I'll mention later some of the kind of resistance training you might want to engage in with your dog, but a "standard" walk shouldn't be a resistance-training maneuver.

A long retractable leash is not suitable for the early stages of walk training. It is best to work with a shorter leash—six feet or less—attached to a collar. While a prong or choke collar can be a useful aid in helping to correct a dog, it isn't necessary. The only correction I recommend when you are working to eliminate a dog from pulling while walking is to immediately stop when you feel tension in the leash and in your arms. That is my negative reinforcement. When you think back about what I said earlier about reinforcement and punishment and Skinner, this simple act best illustrates the point I was trying to make. By stopping, you are taking something good away from your dog—the ability to move forward and the opportunity to do something that he really wants: to sniff, to explore, to mark territory, and so on. You are not inflicting any true physical pain on him. You are not shouting or sternly using words to express your displeasure with him or to somehow admonish him or "shame" him. You are asserting your authority, reminding him who is in control. You're also saying very clearly to the dog, using body language and a kind of kinesthetic statement—the language of movement and how our bodies relate to one another in space—that what he was doing before you stopped was not acceptable.

Stop. Wait. Move on. More pulling. Stop.

Repeat as necessary.

I know that sounds simplistic, but it works. I have yet to work with a dog—regardless of how energetic or how strong his prey drive—who can't or didn't get this message. I don't use any kind of verbal expressions or hand signals to pair the stopping with some other kind of traditional command. I not only stop, but I make it clear by being indifferent toward the dog, acting as if he doesn't even exist, that stopping is the only thing that's going on in that moment. He's not going to get a reward. He's not going to get a legitimate punishment. We're simply ceasing the activity we were engaged in, one that he desired to be engaged in.

This is where that mismatch I mentioned during the selection criteria comes into play. You have to be physically capable of restraining your dog. That may mean that you have to try other kinds of training devices—prong collars, electric collars, or something other than a web collar and a leash. Being able to physically stop your dog is not just necessary for having enjoyable walks to get good exercise. It is a safety issue for you, your dog, and others. If you aren't capable of bringing your dog to a halt to prevent him from going into traffic or from approaching other dogs and people, then that's not a dog you should own or at least not be training yourself.

Of course, stopping once won't get the lesson driven home immediately or permanently. That's where the whole idea of starting early with a dog, working patiently and repetitively, and keeping your emotions in check come into play. Occasionally, with dogs who will pull very hard, I'll use a quick pop on the collar to reinforce the stop.

Dogs are simple-association animals, so eventually the point becomes clear: tension = stopping. That's when a dog's desire kicks in. He wants to walk, to be able to move forward and investigate some smell—in other words, walking = seeking and smelling—so he puts that association together with the tension association and you have the desired behavior nailed. Dogs will figure it all out fairly quickly, but when you start adding in vocalizations and hand gestures and your own anxiety and frustration, you're putting way too much else into the scenario for the dog to sort through.

I've also heard that some people, mainly those who have adopted dogs who weren't properly leash/walk trained, have had good success in curbing overpulling dogs by placing them in a halter. Dogs are very sensitive to touch as a part of their highly developed body language. Any kind of restraint you place on them—a harness touches a dog's chest, shoulders, and back—will work as a kind of restriction. I'm not an advocate for these devices, as it can change the gait/movement of the dog, and ultimately isn't addressing the real issue. Having one device, such as a prong collar that you can use to correct any behavior, makes things simpler for you and for your dog. I will always prefer that training rules the day and the dog. Don't let the device substitute for having command of yourself or control of your dog. The harness will be controlling your dog and not you—and that's not what we're after.

Solve the problem; don't just settle for a quick fix that ends up more long-term than initially intended.

ESSENTIAL FITNESS

We often read about how remaining stationary for several hours per day over long periods of time has detrimental effects to our life expectancy and general health. I don't know exactly how our numbers compare to a dog's, but many dogs are inactive for most of the day, and it is not much better for them than it is for us.

Again, using your situational awareness, you can put together an action plan to counterattack the problems associated with your dog's more sedentary lifestyle. There is no stated amount of steps per day your dog should take (especially since dogs are built with more variance than humans and have four legs), but noting your dog's overall mental and physical condition, and knowing with some precision what his ideal weight is and how much activity keeps him calm and happy, you can experiment with walks of various lengths. As is true of any fitness program you might put yourself on, a couple of things are important to keep in mind.

- Start slow/small/short. Too much too soon leads to injury and is the ultimate case of one step forward, two steps back.
- Eventually a dog's body, like your own, will adjust to the demands placed on it. Continuing to do a regular workout of the same distance and intensity certainly won't hurt your dog, but you won't build his cardiovascular endurance or muscle.
- Variety not only reduces boredom but increases motivation and enthusiasm.
- Dogs, like humans, have different levels of interest in being outside and exercising. Most dogs do like to be active, but there are rare exceptions. I've seen some dogs lose interest in food when not exercised, while other dogs become hyperactive when cooped up too long.
- It's great to be dedicated, but adjust for environmental extremes and understand that periods of rest are an important part of building and maintaining fitness.

FETCHING FOR FUN AND FITNESS

Since seeking is such a big part of a dog's natural life, pursuing thrown objects of any kind is one of the most efficient means of building your dog's physical and mental wellness. This is the best

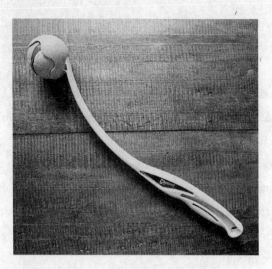

The Chuckit! brand ball and throwing wand is my preferred exercise toy when working with my dogs.

example of a purposeful exercise that you can do with your dog. Not only does any kind of activity with your dog help build your bond, but this kind of catch-and-release activity helps you to establish more command and control. For many dogs, retrieving a ball is a lot of fun. Getting that dog to release the ball is another matter.

When playing fetch for fitness, a couple of things to consider are the length of the throws and the number of repetitions or duration of the exercise. Again, you have to start small and slow and build up to longer tosses, a greater number of repetitions, and the number of times per day or per week you engage in the activity.

PULLING YOUR WEIGHT

Many dogs enjoy pulling things. Sled dogs spring to mind immediately, and I know that in some areas of the country where snow is plentiful, *skijoring* is a popular activity. *Skijoring* is derived from the Danish word for "driving"—think of a dog musher "driving" the dogs. In this case, though, the dogs pull a person wearing cross-country or other types of skis. Training centers, competitions, and trails for the activity are dotted around the country. I'm not suggesting that this is an activity you can or should engage in. But it's important to note that you are allowing your dog to pull in this instance. For some dogs, making the distinction between when pulling is acceptable and when it's not may be difficult. Repetition is the key.

Also, many people and dogs enjoy agility training. Many resources on agility training are available online and elsewhere. Most any dog can do it, and if you are willing to put in the time and attention to get involved, it is a wonderful way to create the kind of bond between you and your dog that most anyone would envy. Dogs like to solve what we might call a puzzle. Exposing them to unknowns and getting them to overcome initial fears and hesitations are all a part of helping their mental development. Going back to the statement at the beginning of the chapter about tired dogs being good dogs, an active and mentally engaged dog is also a good dog. A bored dog can often become a

problem dog because his active brain will lead him to do
something to relieve his boredom.

Be mindful of the environmental conditions and monitor your
dog's panting and his tongue. Since fetch is a kind of sprint, your
dog's heart rate and respiration rate will go up considerably. There
are too many variables in a dog's size and relative health status to
give you anything other than broad ranges for heart rate and pulse,
and these numbers reflect what those norms for are for dogs at rest:

Respiration Rate at Rest: 10–34 breaths per minute

Heart Rate: 60–100 for large breeds

100–140 for small breeds

I generally don't check a dog's pulse or respiration rates while
he's exercising. The one marker that I do pay close attention to is the
tongue. Since dogs cool themselves by exposing their tongues, it is
normal for that tongue to hang out of their mouths. When the
exposed tongue starts to curl back on itself and looks like a soup
ladle, that's an indication that the dog's cooling system is starting to
be overtaxed. That doesn't necessarily mean that you should immediately cease the activity, but modify it in some way to allow the
dog's body to return to a more comfortable state. Obviously, providing water will help cool the dog down. Be careful not to let him
drink more than a few laps, as too much water while exercising

can come back up hastily or can present other digestion/bloat problems.

Just as you would structure your own workout time, having a brief warm-up and cool-down time sandwiched around the main activity will help prevent abuse of your dog's joints and muscles. The same is true of the surface on which you engage in fetch. Concrete is about the hardest surface your dog can run on, so factor that into the length of the session. Twenty minutes is a good amount of playtime on a softer surface like grass, but it may be too much on concrete or other very hard surfaces. Grass or other soft surfaces are ideal for fetch and other sprint activities.

THE NAVY SEAL CANINE WAY

The military working dogs that I train are far more athletic than your typical housepet, but just as a professional athlete uses some of the same training principles as a weekend warrior does, the same is true for canines. I spend a lot of time throwing or chucking balls for all of my dogs. One of the rewards that we use for dogs who successfully identify the location of a chemical compound or complete some other task is to let them have a tennis ball. In fact, most handlers carry a tennis ball or similar reward with them while on an operation and use it for the dog to gnaw on or to fetch.

We also use the pursuit-of-an-object activity as a way to do something called *interval training*. Your dog will most likely alternate between high-intensity and low-intensity movement naturally. He might tear off after a ball or other object, seize it, and then return at a more leisurely pace. That's what interval training is all about—varying the intensity of the effort. Of course, we don't just have the dogs do wind sprints like that all the time. Often, the "object" that the dogs are pursuing isn't an object but a person. Wearing either a bite sleeve or a bite suit, a handler/trainer works with a dog on his tackling, subduing, and fighting techniques. This isn't something I recommend you do with your housepet. In a moment you'll get to the section on playing tug-of-war with your dog and how that's enough to satisfy his requirements for bite work/strengthening.

In addition to interval training, we also work on *endurance training*. We cover long distances in which the dogs are running, trotting, and walking. Those distances vary, as does the terrain we cover and at what altitude we are moving, all to help increase the efficiency of the transport of oxygen to the muscles. Depending on the dog's age and level of fitness, he may engage in interval training, endurance training, and resistance training all in a single day. At the end of this chapter, I'll provide you with a typical workout schedule that you can modify to work with your dog.

As its name implies, *resistance training* means working against a force that is preventing you from moving forward easily. We often place the dogs in a harness and have them drag a tire or some other weight behind them. The weight and friction of the tire dragging along the ground increase the load of resistance and the dog has to work harder in order to make forward progress. The main intent of this is to help build muscle mass, though certainly cardiovascular efficiency is also a part of it.

Maybe it's because I did this as a kid, when having Bud pull me around the neighborhood while I was on a skateboard or

Rollerblades, but harnessing a dog's capabilities like that still seems thrilling and satisfying. I wasn't going to attain supersonic speeds, so it was kind of a low-level thrill, but Bud could get me up to speeds I wasn't able to attain on my own.

As a rule of thumb, I'd suggest that your dog drag something that weighs 10 percent of his overall body weight. I've used metal chains, tires, and other objects to achieve that percentage. If you want to increase that amount of weight, do so gradually and be even more vigilant in observing your dog's condition. Muscle strength is good, but be careful of damage to soft tissue and joint abuse.

In my mind, a perfectly fit dog is one who is strong, possesses great speed, and is capable of great endurance. Working through those three training modalities will give you a dog who is fit overall. I don't think that a dog who excels in one dimension is as valuable or useful as one who is capable in all three areas.

TUGGING AND TEMPERAMENT

I remember hearing someone from my past saying, "Don't let that dog pull on things. It makes him mean." I also heard a variation on this that it was okay to let a dog pull from side to side, but if you allowed up-and-down pulling it would make the dog mean.

I don't know exactly what those people meant by using the word *mean* in those instances, and I don't want to be mean, but that's just nonsense. As I stated earlier about aggression and how that term gets abused, I'd have to say the same things about the myth that playing tug-of-war could turn a dog mean.

For the military working dogs I helped train, probably the reward they wanted most was to bite something or someone. That was good, since detaining a bad guy was one of their main missions. The only way they could do that was by using their mouths. We spent hours working to strengthen their bite. As I mentioned in the previous chapter about your dogs' health, checking their mouths is important because dogs' mouths play so many roles in their lives. Most dogs derive pleasure from chewing things, retrieving things, and carrying objects in their mouth. They lick one another's mouths from their youngest days, similar to how they tried to get their mother to regurgitate food for them. The list of reasons for why a dog's mouth holds so much value for him goes on and on, but primarily today, playing tug-of-war with your dog reenacts what dogs once did in fighting for resources. That could sometimes be serious, but it is also a very natural part of their play with littermates.

Playing tug-of-war with your dog is something you should only do after you've established a strong and trusting relationship. Tugging can reenact competition for resources. Once you've established that you are the one in command and you initiate the activity to signal that you're in charge, then it is acceptable. Use your common sense and if your dog shows signs of being overly possessive, don't promote that by engaging in this activity.

You can buy many kinds of tug toys or make your own (I've used a piece of fire hose stuffed with rags, for example). An important consideration is that it be strong enough to resist tearing too easily, but not so hard that it damages the teeth. Let the dog grab hold of it, then do some pulling from side to side and up and down. Pull the dog. Let him pull you. All of this will help strengthen the neck and jaw muscles, and that kind of exercise is a great stress reliever. It also provides him with some positive chewing experiences. I believe that dogs who get to do their chewing in a structured environment are far less likely to do destructive chewing in and around the home. Also, your dog will know the difference between pulling you when you are engaged in tugging and when you are walking.

A FEW FINAL THOUGHTS ON EXERCISE

I don't take a wholly scientific approach to exercising my dogs— either my personal dogs or ones I train for personal protection or military service. By that I mean that I don't have them attached to heart rate monitors to make sure that they are working at some percentage of their upper limits so that each workout is optimizing the time spent. People who train greyhounds may do that, and so may others who are training for very specific purposes, but I go back to what I've said before about situational awareness. For your housepet, observe your dog and don't push him when he seems to be having an off day. Don't stick to a routine for the sake of a routine.

Keeping your dog fit should be fun for both of you. It should be stimulating mentally, so throw in lots of variation. If you live in the city or suburbs, you may not like this idea, but matching what a dog does in nature to some form of exercise is a good idea. I know people who hide or bury objects (bones, balls, or other items) in snow piles, dirt piles, and other places. They have dogs with good noses and a desire to dig, and they encourage their dogs to find those objects. I've seen these dogs tear into those piles, and if you don't think that's a good workout, get down on your hands and knees and try scratching away feverishly with your hands for a minute or two. Of course, you probably don't want your dog tearing up your lawn or your flower beds or your garden, so allowing your dog to dig is also one of those command-and-control issues.

This kind of "exercise" is ideal because those dogs are doing what comes naturally to them; they are working their brains as well as their bodies, and if you're right there with them, pointing to spots, encouraging them, and just spending time near them, you're strengthening the bond between you.

For most human/canine teams, walking is sufficient. It is a good low-impact way to get exercise. It is your job to be the judge of your dog and his energy level and fitness requirements. If exercise is all about weight management, then walking is the best way to get your dog fit enough for more strenuous kinds of activity. Swimming is another remarkably efficient calorie-burning way for dogs to lose weight, keep the cardiovascular system fit, build muscle, develop better endurance, and, for a lot of dogs, provide an opportunity to do something they love. Not all dogs take to water as some do, and the same principles apply with swimming. I wouldn't necessarily force a dog to do something he is reluctant or unwilling to do. With a pup or a dog who is new to water, gradual exposure and keeping the experience positive will help him adjust and get comfortable.

Take seriously the idea of a cooldown as well. Just as it isn't good for you to engage in strenuous activity and then immediately become sedentary, it isn't good for your dog either. A slow walk after heavy activity, then moving into a shaded area for a brief bit of reclining, contributes to helping a body rid itself of cellular debris more efficiently. Also, proper hydration is essential. Do not let your dog eat or drink too much before or after strenuous exercise. Dogs will vomit more readily if their bellies are full of water while exercising, and that will contribute to dehydration and put you into a nasty cycle of giving them water, exercising, vomiting, needing more water, and so on. Similarly, if you allow them to drink immediately after a hard run or romp, they may consume as many as three, four, or five cups of water. It could easily come back up or, worse, contribute to bloat. Bloat is a problem within the dog's digestive tract. Gases build up too quickly in the stomach, and it inflates. It stretches so much that normal circulation is impaired and eventually cuts off circulation to the heart. Also, when the stomach is stretched and denied blood, some of its cells can die. The worst cases of bloat result in the stomach not just stretching but twisting. That is a very serious condition when a portion near the esophagus and at the bottom are both constricted. As a result, gas is unable to escape from either end and the stomach inflates, causing cellular damage and circulation issues. Shock and then cardiac arrest can follow within an hour or so.

If you notice your dog's belly inflating or tightening excessively, what medical professionals often refer to as *distending*, get him to the vet immediately. A dog's chest will expand during breathing but not the area below the rib cage—that's where you need to focus your attention and your touch. A hard and very enlarged belly is a sign of bloat. That will also be accompanied by your dog showing clear signs of being in some kind of distress—not wanting to move or walk, and so on.

One way to avoid having water intake contribute to this

condition is to wait for your dog to stop panting before providing water. The movement of the stomach during hard panting, during rapid consumption of water, may contribute to bloating and twisting.

Lastly, I can't emphasize enough the mental benefits for you and your dog getting out and being active together. Dogs who are crated all day, many of whom want and need the sense of security it provides, don't get the opportunity to move about freely. Again, if you place yourself in your dog's position and point of view, you'd likely get a little stir-crazy from being cooped up like that. I also think that many dogs enjoy being outside. Don't forget the kind of stimulation that comes from being able to smell, hear, and view a rich natural environment. You may not think that staring out on a street scene is a whole lot of fun, but when you've got a nose that picks up a nearly infinite variety of smells, ears that can pick up sounds from a great distance, and eyes that detect motion and pick out objects in low light and at a great distance, even being out in a fenced-in pen or run is a bit of adventure. Why do you think that when the keys come out, the leash gets grabbed, and door gets opened, it's like Christmas Day for your dog? It has to feel good to be able to give him a well-deserved present as often as possible.

EIGHT

Transforming *Won't* into *Can* and *Does*

Before I address some of the most frequent issues that arise that make a dog owner unhappy, let me reiterate the foundational principles of my training philosophy. If you build a trusting relationship with your dog, and if you establish and carry yourself as the team leader, and if you use the positive system of rewards I've described, then far more often than not, you will experience no real problems with your dog, be able to nip potential problems in the bud, see aggravating issues dissipate over time, and be able to address any long-term issues by going back to the basics.

There are rare cases of owners who have never engaged in formal so-called obedience training with their dogs. They have wonderful relationships with those animals, the dogs have never been destructive or disruptive, and they have good manners and perform the five basic behaviors—sit, stay, down, heel, recall—when prompted. What's the secret? As far as I can tell, it's a matter of that individual having the time and patience to spend a lot of time with the dog, building a trusting relationship. Not all, but most of the people I know like this either are retired, work from home, are childless, or otherwise invest a lot of time and attention in their dogs. Those dogs are active, often engage in some kind of formal exercise or activity like agility trials, and spend a lot of time outdoors, and their owners subscribe to the notion of a tired dog being a good dog.

However, most of us do not have the luxury of being able to spend that much time with a dog, and frequently a dog's misbehavior is as much an expression of his being bored or understimulated with time and attention as it is a lack of intelligence or "trainability," or willfulness. Just as frequently the dog perceives a lack of leadership in the environment. A few times, I've seen dogs kept as housepets who defy the odds for whatever reason and are just stubborn, recalcitrant, free-spirited, defiant, disobedient, or whatever term their owners choose to describe that dog's personality. That doesn't mean that the dog in question can't be trained; it just means that his owners will have to be more patient, raise the level and intensity of their authoritarian demeanor, or, more likely, some combination of both.

For most of these scenarios, I'm going to present a "My dog can't/won't" followed by a "You have to do" structural framework. The first of these is the most general of the bunch, but it also comes up the most frequently.

MY DOG WON'T LISTEN TO ME

Unintentionally or not, the terminology that people use to present their case to me about a dog "not listening" is the culprit. The word *listen* reveals a bias toward verbal communication. It also reveals an incomplete understanding of what your ultimate goal should be—for your dog to react and not simply listen. The sounds your dog hears should trigger that spontaneous muscle response.

One of the reasons why a dog won't present any kind of positive responses to commands is that the hierarchical nature of the relationship has been inverted. If people who have this problem were really honest with themselves, they would instead say, "My dog is in charge of me." (And sometimes they do say that.) But a dog is in charge of an owner only when the owner allows that to be the case. You didn't establish your authority or assume the role of team leader effectively.

How can you fix that?

You Have to . . . start with yourself and how you carry your body. I don't know how many of you have fired a weapon before, but you've likely seen photographs of a soldier or someone else highly trained in weapons fire. That aggressive shooting posture is what you need to adopt for yourself when working with a dog who just won't "listen." You have to communicate to the dog through your body language that you are focused on him and him alone. Think stoic, think regal, an arrogance about you that makes you take the approach that you are allowing the dog to be around you. Also, imagine the stance that a predator takes when it sees its prey. Add to that direct and fierce eye contact, keeping your hips, shoulders, and knees square to the dog, and then advance on that dog.

Another way to think about this is to go back to your days as a child when you had to deal with an annoying sibling or classmate. Either you did this to someone else or you had it done to you. For the purposes of this explanation, let's assume that you were the one who was being more assertive. To really annoy that other person, you encroached on his personal space. You didn't make body contact, but you got close enough to make that person feel uncomfortable. You probably also added some sound to let that other person know when they were doing something you didn't want them to do. It was almost as if the two of you were dancing but still not making any physical contact with each other. You played the stare-down game as well.

That's one way to imagine what it is like to put pressure on a dog who needs to learn who is in charge. You're not shouting; you're not making threatening gestures as if to strike him; you're not thrusting your limbs out at the dog. You're just making it clear that you are in control of how that dog is going to be able to move. For most dogs, that will be enough of a body language signal to send.

Obviously, if you see any sign that the dog is backing down, then you soften your stance and reward his behavior by taking most of the pressure off him. Don't back the dog into a literal corner or to the point when you see him baring his teeth, his hackles rising, or any of the other warning signs that the dog is in fight-or-flight mode.

If that doesn't work, then you have to amplify your approach slightly. This means moving from being a strong presence to having more of a predatorial stance. You have to exude confidence and forward pressure, but that doesn't mean that you physically strike the dog. It is all about how you carry yourself. The pace of your movements will quicken. The volume and intensity of the sounds you might make will increase. Again, you don't shout and express anger, but you do have to send a signal that you are the one in control.

In other words, you have to use your body to bully the dog. I know the major negative connotations associated with that word, but in reality, your dog is bullying you if he doesn't respect you and chooses to act on his own desire. You're not going to get a bully to respond to logic, but you can put physical pressure on him to get him to back down and to relinquish command to you. Remember that dogs understand body language, so your posture/stance and moving toward him to occupy his personal space means a great deal. Your body language should be overbearing.

If you don't notice a change in the dog's demeanor when you become an annoyance—his ears going flat, his eyes becoming downcast, or some other signal that he is surrendering control to you—then continue your advance and make contact with the dog. I don't mean kicking at him, but rather using just the side of your knee to nudge the dog, to put pressure on him, to literally back him against some structure or object. All the time you should keep that intent gaze and expression, but there's no need to say anything verbally. If you need to tell anyone anything, tell yourself that you are the one in control. You're not angry. You're not frightened. You're not fed up. You're just in control.

Ideally, by this point the dog has surrendered. It is important to remember that this maneuver is a last resort. If the dog still shows some kind of defiance—by walking away, moving to avoid your leg, or giving any other indication that the battle is still on—you need to respond in kind and keep the pressure on. If you have the dog on leash, a quick pop and tug qualifies as added pressure on the dog.

At the first sign that the dog is relenting, back off most of the pressure immediately. Soften your stance and relax your gaze. Pet the dog. Say "Good boy." Do what you need to do to let the dog know that you've accepted the terms of the surrender agreement. Taking the pressure off the dog is a reward. Depending on the dog, how long the problem of disobedience has persisted, and to what degree the pressure has taken a toll on the dog, you may want to use other rewards.

If the situation reverts to the old way of being with the dog in charge, you may have to repeat this process several times until the dog completely understands that a transfer of authority has taken place. In some advanced cases, you may need to involve some form of positive punishment, but I would resort to that only if absolutely necessary. As always, use your ability to read your dog to assess the situation. You don't want to put so much pressure on the dog or appear so menacing that you trigger a fight-or-flight response (remember Bob and Rudy). What you want to achieve is the dog's recognition that the only thing he is in charge of in this case is whether the pressure/punishment ends.

In this scenario, and in almost every other one, you might think that something like a time-out you use with children is effective.

It's not.

To me, and more important the dog, there is an enormous difference between removing the problem and solving it. Putting your dog in his crate or banishing him in another room behind closed doors for barking at guests or squirting him with water to silence him ends the event but not the problem. Establishing trust and authority and positively reinforcing what you want to be repeated and ignoring or punishing what you want to extinguish will end the problem. Don't act out of desperation and a desire for an easy solution. Another example is where the dog tries to grab something you don't want him to. Most people have the attitude of "Well, I just won't give him access to it, then"—removing the problem.

The issue with this is that it isn't addressing the root cause of why the dog is going after that object in the first place. You have not taught him the boundaries of what is acceptable in your house. Here is how I deal with this type of scenario: First grab the object and put it in your hands. Hold it at your side naturally and walk toward the dog. Use your body to "bully" him away from you, and keep the object as you would just naturally hold it. Stand so that it is right in front of his face, and if he tries to grab it give him a verbal correction (I often use the sound "Ahhts," but any short harsh sound will do) and bully him back again. Continue this process until the dog will not even acknowledge that the object exists anymore. Once you get the dog to respect this, then try the same techniques with the object on the ground, in the yard, and so on. Communicate with your body that it is unacceptable to grab anything unless you give it to him.

You can head this problem off at the pass if you establish a boundary very early on by having only one or two toys that are specifically your dog's—a ball and some other kind of chew toy. Again, begin by having those items available to the dog outside only. As the dog matures and understands better the unless-I-give-it-to-you-you-can't-have-it concept, then you can relax a bit on that rule. As I write this, my housedog Rico is lying by my side, contentedly chewing on a rubber Kong ball. He knows that ball is his and keeps his mouth off everything else.

MY DOG WON'T COME TO ME
WHEN I CALL HIM

Obviously this is one case when body language doesn't play as much of a role as with the other scenarios. In most cases of failure to recall, the root of the problem lies in how the training was executed. Most dogs will recall when distractions are at a minimum. That means that when working with your dog in that designated training space, you moved on because they were recalling to your satisfaction. In the dog training world, we use the terms *under distraction* and *proofing*. If you don't spend enough time, and I'm talking about dozens of repetitions of a dog recalling successfully in different environments with different levels and types of distractions, then your dog's recall skills will be lacking. Think of when you most want your dog to recall—when he either poses or faces a potential risk. That will seldom occur in a neutral environment.

You Have to . . . build up scenarios with as many real-world distraction factors as possible. Also, don't move from neutral to heavy distraction immediately. Gradually increase the number and types of distractions.

By doing what may seem to you to be excessive numbers of repetitions, you will be building muscle memory in your dog. It will become a reflex response. He hears the command, sees you gesturing, and automatically comes back. Depending on the dog, this may take dozens or hundreds of repetitions at any stage of the recall work.

In terms of reinforcement, you have to give the dog a reason to come back. Remember the principle of flooding—giving many rewards instead of just a single one to drive home the point that a particular behavior has more value. Use flooding if recall is a tough thing for your dog to do regularly. Think of it as a game of poker, in which your hand has to be better than what the dog has. That means he has to earn a reward or he needs to avoid a consequence.

Remember that you have to baby-step everything and provide frequent rewards. Start with the dog three feet away and get him to recall with click and reward. Do this many times and then back up a few feet and repeat. Eventually, if you take this baby-step approach, firmly cement that association, and pair it with a command, when you say "Here" (or make whatever verbalization you've assigned to that task), your dog should come running to you even if he can't see you, even if you are two rooms away indoors or separated by obstacles outdoors. Do as many variations on recall as you can think of and click and reward success.

As with the generally-doesn't-listen worst-case scenario presented earlier, there may be some element of a lack of trust or respect in the relationship that causes a reluctance to recall. If this is just one of two or three issues you're having with the dog, that's not likely to be the case. You don't want or need to go into the kind of bully mode I said was necessary for the dog who felt like he was in charge. Always think in terms of appropriate and reciprocal responses. You're not interested in heightening tensions or damaging the relationship you've worked so hard to build.

Once you've determined that the hierarchy is in place and your authority isn't in question, the last thing you want to do is give your dog a reason to not trust you, respect you, and like being with you.

MY DOG WON'T STAY OFF THE FURNITURE

First of all, placing things on a space to block the dog from going there isn't a solution to the problem. Second, if you are successful in using the "place" command, then you should be able to solve the problem by retraining your dog to go to an alternate location to lie down.

Why your dog wants to be in a specific location despite your numerous efforts to remove him is partly a mystery. The obvious answer is that the reward—being comfortable—is greater than the consequence. You can try to read other things into this, but the reason I just gave (comfort is greater than consequence) is the one that you have to deal with, regardless.

You Have to . . . go through the clicker training routine again to relearn the "place" command. You can start with the dog on the couch, and by using either luring, a leash, or just the "place" command and a point, get the dog off the couch. Once he's got four on the floor, click and reward. Shape the behavior until your dog is lying someplace that you find acceptable. Your dog can and will learn what furniture or locations are acceptable to be on and which ones aren't simply by rewarding him in the places that are okay to be in and not rewarding him in other off-limits areas. As is true with all these behaviors, depending on the dog, you may have to use some punishment. Keep in mind the principles of flooding and repetition as well.

MY DOG WON'T STOP JUMPING
UP ON PEOPLE

Somewhere along the line, you failed to establish a clear association in your dog's mind that this action is a negative one. Remember that behaviors that are rewarded/reinforced get repeated. Here's where your situational awareness and problem-solving abilities have to come into play. Visualize the scenario of the dog jumping on you, your kids, or anyone else, and try to determine how your dog might associate your response or other people's responses to that action as a reward. What is the dog getting that makes him want to do that more than he wants to avoid being punished?

Is it attention? Is it a way to exert his belief that he is in charge? Are people somehow signaling to him through their body language that it is okay for him not to respect their personal boundaries? Does this undesired behavior fit into a larger scheme of other ways the dog doesn't conform to expectations? That may sound like a lot of psychology, but it's not. You're simply doing what you need to do to assess any situation.

You Have to . . . look for patterns. You're not trying to figure out why the dog is doing these things. You're trying to figure out at what stage in the process of developing your relationship with this dog did this aspect of his behavior go off the rails.

If it is an issue of authority, then you have to be even more confrontational than you would in simply preventing the dog from making contact with your body in that way. I've already covered how to go about establishing clear authority. In the moment, effecting a

Use your body gently to get the point across that jumping up is unacceptable.

Get the jump on the dog, the earlier the better, when blocking him from jumping up.

positive punishment by blocking a dog with a knee to the chest or otherwise preventing him from placing his body on yours is step one. Don't allow the behavior to reach the point where the dog is satisfied with the outcome. Thwart him. Be consistent in thwarting him.

Outside the context of him jumping on a person, there are other things you can do. As always, the strong verbal correction you've decided on, whether it's *no* or some other sound, has to be accompanied by strong body language. You must move toward the dog. As always, this shouldn't be an over-the-top charge and highly emotional shout. Clear. Direct. No-nonsense.

MY DOG WON'T GO INTO HIS CRATE

First, I think that a crate is a very good thing to use early in a dog's life or early in his experience with you. It provides him with a neutral spot, a place where he generally can't self-reward and he can't get into much trouble.

You Have to . . . use a combination of rewards and shaping to get your dog into the crate, similar to what you would do with the elevated bed and the "place" command. Like all parts of a dog's experience with you, the initial crating should be a positive one. Most times when a dog develops an aversion to going into the crate, it is because he no longer associates that place with a positive. Using the crate as a kind of time-out zone isn't effective training. Not only does it not address the real issue of solving the problem, it can break the positive association with that location that you and your dog previously built. If that's the case, then you need to repeat what you did earlier in crate training the dog. With enough repetitions of marking and rewarding that behavior, the issue should go away.

For older dogs who come from shelters or other rescue situations, if you don't know the dog's history, experiment with placing him in a crate the first few days, using the same positive-association techniques you now know. Keep the time in there brief; get the dog out often and take him outside and let him know right out of the gate that you are a source of all good things. If a shelter dog shows heavy resistance or aversion to being crated, he may already have some negative associations with it. Take the same steps to associate the crate with positive reinforcement, the same way you need to with anything else you need/want the dog to be able to be around.

MY DOG WON'T GIVE ME THE BALL/TOY BACK

I know that this one frustrates a lot of dog owners, and when it comes to problems it's not very high on the scale of potentially dangerous scenarios. But it does have larger implications that I'll get to. For now, let's just stick with problems playing fetch.

I've briefly touched on this before in talking about Toby and how I would use two balls with him. Professional trainers refer to this as two-balling.

You Have to . . . begin playing fetch as you normally would. When your dog refuses to return the ball to you, simply ignore him. That way you're not meeting any potential need for attention, giving him the thrill of being chased (which many dogs like) or otherwise providing any kind of reward for possessing that ball.

Take out the second ball and make a display of it—toss it in the air, bounce it, and make that ball more appealing than the original one. (This works on a dog's prey drive. The ball in his mouth is "dead" prey. The ball that is moving is alive and is consequently, for most dogs, more enticing.)

Next, turn your back on the dog and walk away. Still toss the ball or in other ways tease the dog and arouse his drive. If he jumps at it, use both your body and your body language to extinguish that behavior. Continue to appear indifferent to your dog, but pay attention very closely to him. As soon as the dog's mouth twitches to release the first ball, reward immediately by clicking (if you're using a clicker) and/or tossing the other ball. Repeat and repeat and repeat.

As with most of these scenarios, the point is to shape the desired behavior first. Get the dog to offer the behavior that you want—releasing the ball. Only after multiple successful repetitions will you add a command or a signal to the training scenario.

Again, timing is crucial. As soon as the dog begins to drop the ball, click, command, and reward.

This is an important behavior to have in place. Dogs who take any object you don't want them to can be trained off that behavior by firmly embedding a "drop" or "out" association in their minds and muscles. As soon as your dog picks up anything you don't want him to, if he's been properly trained with a release command, he should react in the same way as he did with a ball. You can work on this scenario with other objects besides balls to make certain that the association isn't limited to just one object.

Many dogs with high food drive will pick up and try to eat things that could be potentially harmful to them. If you do your due diligence work with other objects, the learning should carry over to even the most tempting treats.

MY DOG WON'T STOP BARKING

Here is where your patience will be tested. I mentioned the family who used "quiet water" earlier. What I did with them most likely was the equivalent of me spraying them in the face with water. They simply had to ignore the dog's barking, wait until he stopped, and immediately reward him when he did. They had to repeat this multiple times and reinforce it whenever the problem recurred.

I know from experience that it is difficult to maintain your patience, but at least you're not having to perform any other action except waiting. Dogs don't bark for no reason, and to expect a dog, whose instincts are telling him to bark to alert us to the presence of a person, an animal, or whatever his senses have detected, to stop is tough.

In training dogs for special operations assignments, we bump into this problem all the time. Throughout our training, the dogs work on apprehending individuals. That means that they have to use their mouths to bite and hold on to an individual. For these dogs, biting something is their greatest reward. They love nothing more. Here's where capping a drive comes into play. When we do clearing operations scenarios, the handler moves the dog into position with the rest of the men. The dog is commanded to lie down.

When the men are signaled that the dog is needed to enter a room and take on a bad guy, he gets released. After a few repetitions of this scenario, the dog starts to make multiple associations. *We all get in a certain formation. I'm commanded to lie down. I get released. I get to bite.*

So, just as your jangling keys get your dog agitated, so do all of those actions. Our dogs bark and whimper and otherwise give away our location. That can't happen.

You Have to . . . break that association and cap that drive. To do that in our clearing operations, we have to not let the dog get what he wants—in our case, that is to bite someone. This is tricky because we do want the dog to understand that his mission is to go into a location and apprehend someone. We just don't want the anticipatory bark. To extinguish that, we employ two scenarios. The first one is just like at home, where we ignore it and let him bark as long as it takes. The instant he is quiet for just a few seconds—*bam!* He is released and rewarded with a bite. Quickly he learns that being quiet and calm means getting his favorite reward: the bite. The second way we can break that association is that as soon as the dog begins to bark, we take him out of line and put him away for a period of time. This disassociates the context and simple association of us lining up and getting him wound up to bark and bite. The same is true for getting your dog to not go crazy when you jingle your keys and the leash; just perform many repetitions of disassociating the two. The difference here of course is that, for us, lives are on the line.

Another alternative both for pet owners and for us is to use a bark collar. This is an electric collar that administers a mild shock to the dog when he barks. I've used one only in rare circumstances as a complete last resort. As a positive punishment, bark collars can be effective, but I use them only if the scenario requires it.

You may find yourself in a situation where you have little choice but to use one. If you have a dog who barks incessantly, who has you threatened with eviction, has neighbors calling the police to file complaints, and so on, then you might consider the use of one. However, I'd suggest one last step before you do that. Call in a professional dog trainer.

Many dogs bark and basically spaz out in the presence of other dogs. To eliminate this behavior, you would use the same process of ignoring the barking and rewarding the quiet. Setting up a training scenario for this presents some logistical problems. I recommend taking your dog to a location where other dogs will be. Keep your barker out of range of the other dogs and on a leash. As before, let the dog bark himself out, then click and reward the calm. Also as before, this will test your patience and the goodwill of others, but it is work that needs to be done. If you register any kind of agitation or embarrassment or frustration, you will prolong the process. Keep your demeanor in check and if your dog's agitation increases, use the body language blocking and command sequences to reinforce the message that calm is the rewarded/desired behavior.

MY DOG WON'T LET ME NEAR HIS FOOD OR OTHER POSSESSIONS

I debated about including this scenario because defensiveness and guardedness are complex issues with an enormous number of variables. I will say two things: First, if you have this problem, you most likely have not developed a proper relationship between yourself and your dog. The trust and respect that needs to be in place is lacking. Dogs who are feeling territorial and lacking in trust should be treated with caution. It is important that you don't address the guardedness in context.

You Have to . . . work on the foundational relationship skills we've talked about instead. Once that proper relationship is in place, the problem should either be eliminated or diminish significantly.

Second, this may be a case where a professional dog trainer can help you eliminate the problem. That is particularly true if the dog presents threatening behavior. This is very much a time when "better safe than sorry" really does apply.

On a related note, I would say much the same thing about a dog who demonstrates neurotic separation anxiety. While the physical threat doesn't typically exist with this problem, at least in most cases, the root cause of a vacuum in leadership is the same. Dogs want and need that authority figure in their lives. In its absence, any number of disruptive behaviors could present themselves.

In all of these troubleshooting scenarios, the simplest truth applies: Get your dog's mind right and the behavior will follow.

Afterword

As I stated at the beginning of this book, the fundamentals that underlie my approach to training a dog are as much about training yourself as your canine companion. Dogs are intelligent animals, but they are looking for leadership and guidance from their owners. They are highly capable team members, but they want and need someone to act as the captain of your two-person team. They are incredibly loyal and lovable, but they thrive best in a relationship that is founded on respect and trust. Many people assume that their dog's devotion and obedience are unconditionally granted, but that's not the case. You have to earn that from your dog. In my mind, the effort that you put in is paid back tenfold in the satisfaction you derive from that relationship. Put another way, you will also have far fewer problems with your dog once you get your mind right, your dog's mind right, and the proper balance in your relationship right.

At their simplest, my methods are all about command and control. You have to be in command of all areas of dog ownership. That means that in selecting a suitable dog, caring for and maintaining your dog's health and general well-being, and tending to all aspects of training a dog to mind his manners, obey directives, and understand the boundaries you place on his behavior, you're the one who has to take command. You control every aspect of that dog's life, but you also have to be in control of yourself. You must be patient. You must be in control of your emotional state. You have to develop a more keen situational awareness. You have to create a vision for the kind of behaviors you want your dog to exhibit, understand and execute plans of action that involve fair and consistent expectations and consequences, and allocate time and resources that maximize your efforts and your enjoyment of being with your dog.

I never look at any aspect of training a working dog or keeping a dog as a housepet as a chore. Yes, there is labor involved, but it is a labor of love. The fact that you got to the end of this book means that you likely feel the same way. There is a huge difference between spoiling a dog and rewarding him as a reflection of and in proportion to how much you benefit from having a dog in your life. Every time I've gone the extra mile with a dog, I've been rewarded.

As I write this, I've just taken a break from having worked again with Toby, the Belgian Malinois I was asked to take on as a kind of rescue project. I'm happy to report that Toby and I have made some real progress in our relationship. We had a few ups and downs, but Toby is at a point now when he looks at his training sessions as a benefit and not as a form of conflict and punishment. I don't really have the words to describe the pleasure I take in seeing Toby use his capabilities to a greater extent than he ever has before. He's in control of his aggressive tendencies, and I can see in his eyes a kind of respect and enthusiasm that was lacking. He is no longer motivated by fear and default aggression but now has a desire to do the things he was bred to do. Toby's exuberance is infectious. I love seeing him work through various training scenarios in which his body exudes a kind of joy in movement that is rare in most people's lives.

We're certainly not all the way there yet, but we're making very good progress. We haven't given up on Toby, and he's starting to show signs that he's come to rely on us not just for taking care of his

Here is the same dog, Toby, relaxed and enjoying the Texas spring weather.

most basic physical needs but as partners who can help him do the kinds of things that he loves.

We employed the principles that I've included in this book. This means that we were able to:

- Look at things from the dog's perspective.
- Appreciate the differences in how dogs use their senses to perceive the world.
- Look at the intelligence behind a mistake.
- Reward good behavior.
- Punish/extinguish bad behavior.
- Reward and punish employing the theories of B. F. Skinner:
  - Something good can begin or be offered.
  - Something good can stop or be removed.
  - Something bad can begin or be offered.
  - Something bad can stop or be removed.
- Be consistent in the application of rewards and punishments.
- Keep emotion out of the evaluation of good and bad and the application of punishments.
- Understand how dogs communicate overwhelmingly through body language and use that understanding and method of communication back to them to elicit the kinds of behaviors that we want.
- Determine our needs and understand how a dog's prey drive, energy level, and other physical traits contribute to a matrix of behavior.

- Provide a dog with ample amounts of exercise and interaction with other dogs and people in a multitude of different environments.
- Feed him a diet with the maximum health benefits within our means.
- Before undergoing formal training, develop a bond of mutual trust and respect.
- Become the authority figure in a dog's life that he wants and needs.
- Employ clicker training to help mark desired behaviors and help the dog to find out how to learn.
- Take the time to be patient, do multiple repetitions, build in different levels of distraction, and employ variable reward schedules, all to ensure that a concept is firmly embedded in a dog's mind.
- Use good problem-solving skills to identify the root cause of a problem and work out a solution to resolve the issue and not just hide it.

This is a quick review of the most fundamental concepts in the book. As I've stated before, an enormous number of variables exist in any dynamic relationship. As a result, I can't possibly give you a step-by-step solution to every behavioral issue that arises. Essentially, you have to do a self-check first. Is your dog not behaving properly because of something that has to do with you and his perception that a lack of leadership exists? If so, then you need to work on the relationship issue before doing any kind of retraining using the best practices and principles laid out here. If the relationship is good and you do have command and control, then it's time to get back into the classroom, evaluate how some fault may have crept into either the teaching or the learning, and refine your method but stick with the fundamental principles.

I hope that you'll soon be able to experience the joy that comes from having a well-mannered and obedient dog. I know that I enjoy a dog's company tremendously, but that sense of satisfaction and connection is even deeper and more rewarding when you are in command and in control of both yourself and the relationship you have with your best friend. When you work hard to bring out the best in your dog, he's helping to bring out the best in you.